The Kiruv Files

The stories, the drama, the humor...
an inside look

Dovid Kaplan
Elimelech Meisels

TARGUM/FELDHEIM

First published 2003
Copyright © 2003 by Dovid Kaplan and Elimelech Meisels
ISBN 1-56871-235-9

All rights reserved

No part of this publication may be translated, reproduced, stored in a retrieval system, or transmitted in any form or by any means, electronic, mechanical, photocopying, recording, or otherwise, without prior permission in writing from both the copyright holder and the publisher.

Published by:
TARGUM PRESS, INC.
22700 W. Eleven Mile Rd.
Southfield, MI 48034
E-mail: targum@netvision.net.il
Fax: 888-298-9992
www.targum.com

Distributed by:
FELDHEIM PUBLISHERS
202 Airport Executive Park
Nanuet, NY 10954
www.feldheim.com

Printed in Israel

June 30, 2003   30 Sivan 5763

Kiruv rechokim is a very serious business. There are heart-wrenching moments and heartwarming ones as you reach into the heart and soul of someone you are trying to help find his way back.

Kiruv also has its light side. Not only does a funny thing sometimes happen to you while you are on the way to success, but you also need a good sense of humor even while expounding on the most serious subject of Torah thought. It is this ingredient which allows the newcomer to appreciate the human element in the mentor so removed from him intellectually and spiritually.

Rabbi Dovid Kaplan is a central figure in a number of the introductory programs at Ohr Somayach and a much sought-after lecturer and writer throughout the world. His ability to spice his erudition with a little humor has endeared him to a generation of students here and audiences everywhere.

"The Kiruv Files" reflects both his style and his experience and will serve as a valuable handbook for people in the Kiruv-field and a wonderful welcome mat for outsiders who wish to return but are hesitant to make the move.

May Hashem grant Reb Dovid the greatest success in seeing this great book achieve its goal of making kiruv something to smile about.

Rabbi Mendel Weinbach
Rosh Yeshiva

SEMINAR YERUSHALAYIM
HâChadash

U.S. OFFICE: 4622 14ᵀᴴ AVENUE ✦ BROOKLYN, NY 11219
(718) 633-8557, FAX: (718) 435-0115 ✦ ss.seminary@verizon.net

RABBI MICHOEL J. MEISELS
DEAN & PRESIDENT

RABBI ZEV LEFF
RABBINIC ADVISOR & LECTURER

MRS. CHANA M. FLAM
MENAHELES
✦
MRS. H. MEISELS
ADMINISTRATOR, U.S. OFFICE

בס"ד

Tammuz 2003
June 2003

Dear Rabbis Dovid Kaplan and Elimelech Meisels, עמו"ש

It is with pleasure and with pride that I am privileged to review and to comment on the "first fruits" of your journalistic labors and to admire your unique style and approach to the demanding area of Kiruv.

While our interest and, in fact, our obligation towards our brethren at every level of observance has become more widespread, there exists more than one approach to success in this noble endeavor.

The famous Chinese philosopher, Confucius, once said, "a picture is worth a thousand words". You have succeeded in drawing a picture *with* words, presenting in script, a very humane, often humorous approach to understanding the complexities of reaching the mindset of the Jew who is searching for meaning in his life, and who responds to the suggestion that Torah provides our people with much more than meaning in life – it provides *life* itself.

חנוך לנער על פי דרכו (משלי) – This נער, this youth, need not be specifically young in years – he may be a נער by virtue of his awakening senses which cry out for anchorage and guidance – he, too, is a נער, one who is experiencing "awakening", which is the root-word of נער.

Reading your book is not only often entertaining, it is decidedly instructive for those whose thinking and concern extend beyond themselves and who feel the anguish of the many in עם ישראל, who are ignorant of our nation's exalted place in creation.

My most heartfelt ברכות of further success are herein extended to you.

בידידות נאמנה,

Rabbi Michoel Meisels
Dean

רח' הרב פרנק 38 ✦ ת.ד. 16285 ✦ ירושלים 91162 ✦ ישראל
בנין הפנימיה: רחוב בית וגן 99א ✦ ירושלים 96426 ✦ ישראל
(02) 643-9303, FAX: (02) 642-2487 ✦ semyeru@barak-online.net

סמינר
ירושלים החדש

In memory of

HaRav HaGaon
Mordechai Shakovitsky, z"l

who provided me
with so much guidance
and direction

יהי זכרו ברוך

For Miri, Ari, Esther Rivka,
Zevi, Batsheva, Chaya,
and Yossie

E. M.

Contents

Preface 11
Introduction 15
The Real Heroes. 21
Faith Healers and Swamp Dwellers 33
Kiruv Questions 49
Parents. 69
Positive Feedback 91
Shidduchim 99
Ouch! You're Shuckeling Too Hard! 115
Unexpected Reactions 125
Under the Influence 135
Those Ultra-Orthodox! 159
Halachic Issues 189
The Philosophers. 207
Uniform Reactions 221
About the Authors 239

PREFACE

It is with gratitude to *Hashem Yisbarach* that we present this book to the English-speaking public.

Several years ago I made cassette recordings of some of my experiences in the field of *kiruv rechokim* and gave them to Rabbi Eli Meisels to transcribe into book form. Knowing that he is remarkably perceptive and a talented writer, I felt he would be the perfect choice to put together a good product. What he has done with these recordings far exceeds the parameters of the word *transcribe*. He has, simply put, written a masterful book. Not only has he expressed my thoughts and feelings in a way that I could not, but he has graciously contributed some of his own experiences in the field of *kiruv* and *chinuch* as well. A strong friendship has been formed as a result of our partnership in authoring this work, and for all of his efforts, I will always be extremely grateful.

Throughout the book there are suggestions on how to approach various issues in *kiruv*. There is strong emphasis placed on the fact that these are my own personal methods, some of which I have learned from my mentors and colleagues and some of which I developed on my own through trial and error. This does not mean that there are not better techniques, arguments, and explanations or that there are not more efficient ways of doing *kiruv*. I hope the ones in this book will be of help to others in the field.

All names and locations whose identities should remain unknown have been changed. Any attempt to identify the person in question will at best result in a coincidental similarity.

There are two types of conversations that appear in the book. Some are almost verbatim accounts of conversations that took place with specific individuals. Others are models of conversations that have taken place countless times with different people. They have been reconstructed here in an attempt to present an approach to dealing with the issue in question.

All stories contributed by Rabbi Meisels are indicated by the initials E. M. which follow them.

While my principle place of involvement in *kiruv* and *chinuch* is Yeshivas Ohr Somayach, the anecdotes and experiences described in the book are gathered from other yeshivos, seminaries, *kiruv* centers, and outreach organizations that I have been privileged to be involved with both in Jerusalem and in cities around the world. All opinions in the book are my own and are not representative of any specific institution.

Throughout the years of my involvement in *kiruv*, my gratitude to HaKadosh Baruch Hu for allowing me to spend my time in this incredibly fulfilling occupation has not diminished. As a matter of fact, it has progressively increased. This book, which will hopefully benefit others in the field of *kiruv* by providing guidance and "learn-from-my-mistakes" advice, is another source of overwhelming feelings of *hakaras hatov* to the *Borei Olam*.

On the subject of *hakaras hatov*, I would like to express my gratitude to a number of people. First and foremost, to my parents, Rabbi and Mrs. Marchal Kaplan, who have provided emotional and material support since the day I was born which has grown exponentially throughout the years. Friends and family alike can attest to the fact that through their warmth and good-heartedness they have drawn close all those with whom they have come in contact. Their life could be described as one thick *kiruv* file. If this book provides them with a modicum of *nachas*, it will have been well worth the effort.

My parents-in-law, Mr. and Mrs. Eugene Cohen, have served as role models for our family. They have taught us what *mentschlichkeit* is all about. May Hashem bless our parents with good health and *nachas* from all their offspring.

It is an honor for me to be able to thank in print the crown of our family, my *bubby*, Mrs. Ethel Greenberg, a living example of a *kiruv* personality. May Hashem grant her many years of good health and *Yiddishe nachas*.

Special thanks to Rav Nota Schiller, *rosh yeshivah* of Ohr Somayach, and to *chavrei hahanhalah*, Rav Yaacov Bradpiece and Rav Michoel Schoen, whose influence, encouragement, and sacrifice have made this book possible.

HaGaon HaRav Mendel Weinbach, *shlita*, has been one of my primary *rebbeim* and advisors over the past couple of decades. He has taught me Torah and he has taught me life. Practically nothing I have done in *kiruv* or *chinuch* has been without his guidance and approval, and this book is no exception. Rav Weinbach read and commented on the entire manuscript, and almost all of his suggestions have been incorporated into the text. No words can do justice to the debt of gratitude I owe to a man who has guided and educated thousands.

Heartfelt thanks to HaGaon HaRav Naftali Kaplan for advising and encouraging me to enter the field of *chinuch* and *kiruv*.

To all the *talmidim* and audiences who have been good enough to listen to my *shiurim* and lectures, I am truly grateful.

Special thanks to the staff of Targum Press for their courtesy and professionalism.

It is my *tefillah* that HaKadosh Baruch Hu should help my wife, my children, and myself to spend our lives serving Him through teaching Torah and *kiruv rechokim* and that we should be *zocheh* to receive His *berachah* in *gashmiyus* and *ruchniyus*.

— Dovid Kaplan

INTRODUCTION

A few weeks ago I was approached by a friend of mine who is a teacher in Yeshivas Ohr Somayach's advanced Center program, and his was a pretty straightforward request.

"Eli, would you mind having two guys from the Center over for a meal on Shabbos?"

I cleared the request with my wife, and we settled on Shabbos lunch. Like many local English-speaking families, we have Shabbos guests on a pretty regular basis. On Shabbos morning, when the boys showed up before I arrived home from shul, my wife greeted them and went into the kitchen to prepare the meal, leaving the guests to entertain themselves until I returned.

Perhaps ten minutes after the guests arrived I came home from shul, and we made introductions all around. It turned out they were both named Daniel, which gave us an opening topic for conversation, and then we settled down to eat.

In the course of the conversation, one of the young men, a pleasant twenty-four-year-old named Daniel Lubin, told me his story.

He had visited Israel once as a teenager, and though he had a nice time touring the country, he did not look for, nor find, any kind of religious experience. When he was twenty-one, he returned to Israel for another visit, again looking for nothing more than a good time.

After several weeks of picking bananas on a kibbutz and some time touring up north, Daniel decided to spend his last weekend in Jerusalem. He would go to the Western Wall on Friday night and drive down to the Dead Sea on Saturday morning.

He spent his time at the Wall observing the black-hatted Jews praying and un-hatted tourists snapping pictures. After a short time, having nothing more to see, he turned to leave.

He never made it.

Meir Schuster intercepted him. "Do you have anywhere to eat tonight? Would you like to experience a real Shabbos meal?"

Daniel was slightly taken aback, but with nothing more exciting than a slice of pizza on the agenda, he decided to go along with the offer. At worst, it would be an interesting story to tell his friends when he got back to the States. And if the food was really terrible, he could always get that slice of pizza later.

Schuster hooked him up with another young man, a hulking Australian bartender traveling around the world, and off they went to experience their first taste of gefilte fish.

"Well," Daniel said to me, "that meal changed my life. I had the most incredible time, the food was great, the conversation was really stimulating, and the singing was beautiful. It lasted until one in the morning, and I knew right then that I had to check out this religion business. I had never felt anything was missing, but now I saw how much more there could be to life."

The next morning Daniel went on his trip to the Dead Sea, and with only twenty-four hours remaining in his visit to Israel, he crammed in a few lectures on Torah and Judaism before flying home Sunday evening.

But something had changed.

Although Daniel had returned to America and his college life, now he felt something was missing. He couldn't forget his incredible experience at that Shabbos table in Jerusalem. As soon as he was able, he sought the local Orthodox community for resources that could help him learn more about his heritage. He was thrilled when he found several knowledgeable and dedicated rabbis who could help him explore his roots.

Under their expert tutelage, Daniel found new vistas opening before him, and he took to it like a fish to water. It wasn't long before he became fully observant and was experiencing for himself the thrill of studying in-depth Torah and living as a Torah-true Jew. Daniel longed to attend a yeshivah and study Torah full-time, but he felt it would be prudent to finish college first.

Finally, having obtained his diploma, Daniel was back in Israel, the place where his adventure had begun three years before, and the circle was now complete.

Almost.

I had listened to the tale with interest and admiration, and now that he had finished, I had only one comment.

I said, "I didn't know Meir Schuster had people over to his own house for meals. I thought he usually sent them to other families. It's interesting that you had the good luck to eat in Schuster's own home."

Daniel said, "No, you misunderstood. I didn't eat with Schuster. He sent me to an American family for the meal."

"Oh, I see. Do you happen to remember who it was?"

"Yes, I do," said Daniel.

"Really? What is their name? I wonder if I know them."

Instead of answering, Daniel pointed at the table.

I looked at him in puzzlement. "What do you mean? Was it someone in this building?"

He nodded.

I started to list the names of my American neighbors.

He shook his head and said, "No, it was in this apartment."

I said, "Really? What a coincidence. Who lived in this apartment three years ago?"

Daniel just smiled.

Well, slow I may be, but finally I caught on. We had been living in this apartment for almost seven years.

"You mean you ate here?"

Daniel nodded.

"Here, with us?"

"Yep!"

"You mean you knew all along? You set up this meal?"

"That's right. I've been wanting to return here for the past three years. And that's why I bought you this little gift. I remembered that we made a *l'chaim*, and you didn't have shot glasses, so I bought you this decanter set to say thank you — for the meal and, well, for everything!"

Now the circle really was complete.

For the first time in a very long while, I was truly speechless. But, to be honest, there was no need for speeches. I just sat there and soaked it in, stunned and happy that I, and my family, had made such a difference in another Jew's life. And with such a small effort.

And that is the real reason I am telling you this story. Not to boast about our wonderful Shabbos meals; if there's anything wonderful about them, the credit goes to my wife, not me. And not just to share an entertaining story either.

I tell you this story because it shows how each and every one of us, professional *kiruv* worker or not, has the ability to utterly change the world. And it does not require tremendous exertion either, but a minimum of effort. How difficult is it to have a guest over on Shabbos and drink a *l'chaim* together?

And if we have the ability to change another Jew's life, then we have the obligation to do so.

That is the point of the story and the primary purpose of this book — to show the "average" *frum* Jew that what he is, and the way he lives, are all he needs to spread the word of Hashem.

It needn't be through a brilliant Torah lecture or a subtle deconstruction of Darwin's theory of evolution. It could be a Shabbos meal or a kind word. It could be an act of integrity or a helping hand. That is all we really need to make a *kiddush Hashem*.

The most amazing thing about this is that we may never know the results of a seemingly insignificant action. Had Daniel Lubin not made a point of returning to our house, we would probably never have known what we had helped achieve, and we would never have gotten the

INTRODUCTION

chizuk and the boost that we did.

I had always claimed that one does not need to be a great scholar nor a trained *kiruv* expert to make someone *frum*. Thanks to Daniel Lubin and a "chance" encounter, now I have the proof that this is true.

I wish to express my gratitude to the *Ribbono shel Olam* for giving me the opportunity to write this book and in general for providing that I be involved in *avodas hakodesh*.

Thanks to Mrs. Esther Schwalbe for her dedicated work on the manuscript.

I must also thank my parents, whose all-encompassing *ne'imus* and *ahavas Yisrael* were for me, and remain to this day, the greatest example of *kiruv*, *rechokim* and *krovim*, imaginable.

Finally, to my wife, Tami, for her patience and graciousness in opening our home to all manner of company on short or no notice. Her wondrous culinary skills ensure that there is never a shortage of *kiruv* opportunities at our table. In fact, truth be told, I have no doubt that her delectable cuisine goes as far, if not further, in being *mekarev levavos* than anything I could possibly say or do.

May it be the will of Hashem that through the stories and ideas related in this book we see our *Yiddishkeit* for the beautiful gift it is. And may we find ways to utilize this gift to affect and inspire our fellow Jews in a positive manner so that they, too, can find their place in the harmonious medley of true Judaism.

— Elimelech Meisels

The Real Heroes

THE REAL HEROES

The world recognizes a lot of heroes, some fictional, as encountered in the movies, and some less fictional, as found in the police, fire departments, and Hatzalah organizations the world over.

For my money, though, the real heroes of today's world are the *ba'alei teshuvah*. They don't just have to perform a single heroic act for a relatively short period of time; they must remake their entire lives, without hope of material reward or recognition and in the face of sometimes overwhelming opposition.

The Talmud says, "*B'makom sheba'al teshuvah omeid afilu tzaddik gamur eino yachol la'amod* — In the place where a *ba'al teshuvah* stands, even the greatest of righteous men cannot approach."

One of the explanations for this is that the challenges a *ba'al teshuvah* faces and conquers for his religion are far greater than those a Jew born to the religious fold deals with. Without having been born to it, they recognize the truth, learn about it, and have the courage to live by their convictions.

A Script for Life

Joe Thorman was a funny guy. Really funny. Sitting in the dining room during lunch, he could have the whole table laughing with a single well-placed word or even only a well-timed facial expression. The Purim play Joe's year was one of the best in Ohr Somayach history.

Joe hadn't planned on these impromptu lunchtime performances. At one time Joe had intended to use his comedic talent, along with his considerable writing skills, in a larger forum than the Ohr Somayach dining room — in the world's largest such forum. Since he had been a small child, Joe wanted only one thing out of life: to be a Hollywood scriptwriter.

For this he sacrificed a great deal. Along with the thousands of other dreamers who descend on Los Angeles yearly and work menial jobs hoping for their big break, Joe Thorman waited tables and dreamed. He dreamed of the one thing that mattered to him: writing scripts for movies.

He didn't want to act in movies; he didn't want to direct movies. He only wanted to write the scripts for movies, and he was convinced he had the talent. He just needed one break. And he knew that once he got that break and sold his first script, once he got into the club, he would be set for life.

Well, Joe waited a lot of tables, but his big break didn't materialize. He didn't give up; he kept writing script proposals, dropping them off at the studios, and harassing every connected person he could reach, begging them to at least read one of his scripts to see if he had the goods to succeed.

At some point during Joe's wait to get rich and famous, he stumbled onto Judaism. He didn't have much else to keep him busy, so he began attending some classes, and slowly he began to realize that there was something missing in his life, something besides a movie-writing contract.

Slowly he found his way back to his roots and became more and more observant, but he still kept his dream of script writing alive. Eventually, realizing that Hollywood wasn't knocking down his door and looking to acquire more Jewish knowledge, Joe decided he would travel to Israel and study in Ohr Somayach for a year. Hollywood would have to wait.

Well, what do you know — all of a sudden Hollywood couldn't wait. The week before Joe was to leave he received a call from the head of a major movie studio; they wanted to produce one of Joe's scripts, and they wanted Joe on board as an in-house writer. He would receive a salaried position and royalties on all his scripts. Best of all, he would live out his dream of writing movies. The break he'd been waiting for all his life had finally come.

Of course, he would have to postpone that year in yeshivah if he wanted to take this job, but there was no rush. He could study Torah any time. This job was a once-in-a-lifetime opportunity. Joe intended to remain religious, and even make a *kiddush Hashem* as a religious, principled Jew in the movie industry. Ohr Somayach would have to wait.

Such was Joe's immediate reaction.

Upon a little reflection, and much consultation with people whom he greatly respected, Joe realized he couldn't do both. His *Yiddishkeit* was nowhere near strong enough to withstand the tests of working in the movies, the very wellspring of the world's immorality.

He knew he was being forced to choose one or the other: his lifelong dream or his religious observance, which had picked up in the last twelve months. An excruciating choice, one with which most of us would hope never to be faced.

After much agonizing, and much serious thought about his life and his goals, Joe came to a decision. He would follow his head, not his heart. Though his lifelong ambition was finally being realized, he would continue with his plans and do what he knew was the correct thing: he would go to Jerusalem and study Torah.

And that was how I found out that Joe Thorman was a funny guy.

Joe had a nonreligious twin brother named Mark. When Joe told him of his decision, Mark cried. He was convinced Joe had lost his marbles.

When Joe first told me his story, I knew one thing for sure: Joe Thorman would always remain true to the Torah. No one sacrifices that much for something to which he isn't fully committed. The very sacrifice helps create and solidify the commitment. Joe had given up his lifelong dream for his tradition; that tradition was now his forever.

The story even has a happy ending. *Baruch Hashem*, Hollywood has survived without Joe Thorman, and as for Joe, well, he's done more than survive. He's thrived as a happy, *frum* Jew and the proud father of six beautiful *Yiddishe kinderlach*.

Trial by E-Mail

Paul Samuels is the type of person people pour their hearts out to — a great listener and a great guy. Everyone thinks of Paul as his best friend.

One day Paul came up to me and showed me a letter he'd received. His friend was getting married and couldn't imagine doing so without Paul at his side; he wanted to fly Paul in for the wedding.

There was a technical problem, though — the young lady he was marrying was not Jewish. Paul asked me what he should do. I sat down with him, and together we composed a letter stating that under the circumstances Paul could not come to the wedding. He could not, in good conscience, attend and celebrate his good friend's interfaith marriage. Paul was careful not to condemn his friend. He just explained that he would not feel right attending the wedding.

His friend wrote back, saying he'd received Paul's letter and he'd picked up a certain disapproving drift in Paul's words, so would Paul please explain, frankly, what the problem was? Paul replied with a very sensitive letter, explaining that by marrying a non-Jewish girl his friend was leaving his faith irrevocably and ensuring that his children would not be Jewish, thus effectively cutting himself off from the Jewish people. He never heard from that friend again.

A few weeks later Paul came back to me with another letter. A former acquaintance of his, a young lady, had been thinking about him and wanted to know what Paul was doing with his life; perhaps they could get back together. Paul wrote back that he was studying in a yeshivah and becoming religious, so he didn't think the relationship was really renewable. Not surprisingly, he never heard from her again either.

A week later Paul came to me with another e-mail, this one from the first girl he had ever gone out with. He hadn't seen her in about eight years. She wanted to know where he was so they could resume their relationship. It was getting rather hilarious; I told him he should just make up a form letter. Once again Paul wrote back that he was in yeshivah, and once again that was the last he heard from her.

So despite the *yetzer hara*'s best efforts to pull him away, and they were impressive, Paul is still in yeshivah, and still learning.

Let's Make a Deal

Paul came by the other day to show me yet another letter. His family consider themselves "Jewish traditional." However, their tradition is a pretty tolerant one — one brother intermarried and has a couple of gentile kids.

It seems the family had been sitting together and discussing how they felt about Paul attending a yeshivah. Being liberal-minded Americans, the consensus was that they didn't mind his being in yeshivah, but then the question arose: what did Paul think of *them*? Particularly, what did he think of his brother's children? Was he as liberal as they, and would he agree to accept Sean and Mary as Jews?

The answer to this question was apparently a matter of some urgency, since his brother immediately wrote him an e-mail inquiring as to what Paul thought of his wife and children, reply requested ASAP. A difficult position for a beginning *ba'al teshuvah* — or, truthfully, for anyone — to be in.

This was the letter Paul brought to show me, and he asked for advice on how to respond. Paul tactfully wrote back that he thought his brother's wife, Theresa, was a very nice person and that his children were adorable, but according to our tradition, they were not Jewish. He e-mailed his carefully crafted reply to his brother, and then he waited. He waited about two weeks, and then he waited some more.

Two months later he e-mailed his brother again, asking if his e-mail was working since he hadn't heard back from him. His brother responded very cordially, but refused to discuss the issue of his marriage. Apparently Paul's reply was not the right one, maybe just a tad too "traditional."

On another occasion Paul told me how he and his family finally managed to come to a relatively happy and peaceful medium. I have since passed this on to many students who are experiencing familial tensions regarding religion.

On a visit to the U.S. Paul had dinner with his three nonreligious brothers, and what began as a pleasant get-together soon turned into a three-on-one religion-bashing session.

Finally Paul said to his brothers in a calm tone, "Look, you are who you are, and you are not going to change. I also am not going to change. If every time we get together you're going to bash me, then I won't be able to come. If you will accept me as I am and want to spend a pleasant time together, I'm more than happy to. Just let me know. It's up to you."

For the most part, it's been effective. Every time one of his family members starts with him, he simply gives a "we made a deal" look, and the matter is dropped.

He may not succeed in being *mekarev* his family, but at least they can get along.

More Precious than Gold

Lior Cohen was a prominent bank manager in the Tel Aviv area. Somehow, despite his completely secular surroundings and lifestyle, he became attracted to Torah and began studying his long-lost tradition. He progressed rapidly in his knowledge and slowly but surely decided to change his lifestyle to a more observant one. He started by keeping kosher and Shabbos and even went out and bought a pair of tefillin, something he hadn't experienced since his bar mitzvah thirty years earlier. He found a synagogue a short distance from his house and began attending regular morning services, where he proudly wore his tefillin. He felt, for the first time in his life, happy and fulfilled and sure of what he was doing.

He did have one limitation. When it came to donning a *kippah*, Lior just could not find it within himself to do so. He was embarrassed in front of his friends, neighbors, and colleagues. As long as he kept his new mitzvah observance kind of private, he didn't suffer too much, but he was afraid of the attitude he would face were he to walk around all day with a skullcap on his head. His acquaintances would think he had gone off his rocker. So, despite feeling somewhat ashamed of his lack of moral strength, the *kippah* was the one thing on which he compromised.

One morning Lior was at work in the bank when a wealthy depositor arrived. He was a distinguished elderly man who had made a fortune in business and later entered Israeli politics, where he left a lasting mark on the country.

He had called earlier and said he was going to come by to deposit a bag of gold coins in his safe-deposit box. He had always kept them at home as a security measure in case of calamity, but now, with his advancing age and the high crime rate, he no longer felt secure at home.

The bank was rather crowded that morning, and Lior watched the man struggling to make his way through the throng, tightly clutching his bag of coins to his chest.

Then disaster struck. A customer in a hurry elbowed another man, who shoved him in the back and right into the elderly treasure-bearer. The bag slipped from his grasp, hit the floor, and burst open. Suddenly there were gold coins all over the floor of the crowded bank.

The distinguished depositor let out a shriek, dropped to the floor, and began scrambling like a madman after his money. With no regard for his station or reputation, he pushed and he clawed, he crawled and he cursed, trying to protect his valuable assets.

Lior ran over to help, as did many of the customers, and soon the man's money was restored to him, and he was ushered into the manager's office to have a drink and soothe his rattled nerves.

All had ended well, but Lior was a changed man. He could not get over the way this distinguished, respected statesman had debased himself in recovering his gold coins. Didn't he have any self-respect? Didn't he care that there were so many people in the bank watching him scrambling wildly on the floor?

Lior thought about it and came to the realization that when a person truly loves something, and truly desires it, there is no shame felt in the pursuit of that thing. This man loved his money, so he didn't hesitate for a second to worry about indignity or the reactions of others. He just went after his money.

And I? thought Lior. *I love the Torah and the mitzvos, yet I am concerned about what a few people might say about my lifestyle. The Torah is compared favorably to gold and silver. Do I really love the Torah so much less than that man loves his money?*

The next day Lior showed up at the bank proudly sporting a *kippah*. No longer did he feel shame in living up to his beliefs, his own precious bag of gold coins.

A Man of Principle

Franz came from South Africa. A sensitive, caring young man, Franz was not the wild, party-hearty type of college kid. When Franz came to Ohr Somayach, he was already on his way to becoming observant, but he still had a friend with whom he felt very close. Like everything about Franz, this friendship was not a childish, puppy-love affair, but a committed relationship, which both parties were hoping would one day lead to marriage.

The problem was this newfound religious interest of Franz's. Unfortunately, his girlfriend was not as interested in Torah Judaism as Franz, and she did not want to commit to living an observant lifestyle. After much soul-searching and careful consideration, Franz came to an agonizing decision. He and his girlfriend would have to end their relationship. He could not compromise his commitment to living a Torah-true lifestyle. It takes only a few lines to set down on paper, but this was far from an easy decision.

As Franz himself told me, he made this resolve not knowing how long it might be before he would meet someone else. He was a serious individual, mature beyond his years, and he knew it would not be easy to find someone as suited to him as his fiancée. But as a person of principle, he believed he could not do otherwise.

Happily Franz eventually settled in England, where he met a nice girl with similar life goals.

Like I said, these are the true heroes.

Faith Healers and Swamp Dwellers

FAITH HEALERS AND SWAMP DWELLERS

One of the fringe benefits of teaching in an institution like Ohr Somayach is the sheer number of high achievers and accomplished professionals with whom one comes into daily contact. The yeshivah is filled with doctors, lawyers, and successful businessmen, all of them engaged in the same pursuit: the intense study of Torah.

Besides the intellectual stimulation these diverse individuals provide, occasionally there is a practical benefit as well. I was once speaking with a student in a private counsel room when my left eye suddenly lost its ability to focus. Everything looked black. I closed my eyes, and my vision returned to normal, but not for long. My ability to focus kept coming and going.

I grew very concerned. This had never happened to me before. I quickly went to the *beis midrash*, where there are always at least one or two doctors hanging around, and one of our resident doctors gave me an on-the-spot eye exam and advised me to see an eye specialist immediately. It turned out that I had a torn retina, which, due to the prompt medical attention, was soon restored.

There is so much talent in Ohr Somayach that whatever specialty a person might need can easily be found. Lawyers, doctors, business professionals, investment counselors — the entire professional spectrum. For any requirement there's an expert available with whom to consult. I'd like to introduce you to a few of them.

Gil Rudinsky from Chicago is a cheerful, unassuming guy whom I've gotten to know from sitting near him in the *beis midrash*. One day I asked him what he did for a living. Casually he answered, "Oh, I'm a physician." While many professionals take pride in their fields and manage to let you know about their level of attainment, I would never have known Gil's unless I'd asked.

Gil is a true example of *"Torah im derech eretz,"* of combining Torah study with earning a livelihood. He travels to America every few months for a period of two weeks, earns enough as an ER night-shift physician to support his family in Israel, and comes back to learn Torah full-time.

Sasha Chernishvilli is Georgian by birth. He came to the yeshivah from the former Soviet Union and quickly made a name for himself as a scholar. The rigorous learning methodology and Talmudic logic appealed to his brilliant mind.

Among his various talents, Sasha is a computer whiz, and he periodically leaves the yeshivah for four to six weeks in order to, as he puts it, "earn amazing amounts of money." Apparently Sasha possesses some special technical skills that enable him to take short-term jobs at his own discretion and earn enough to support himself and his family the rest of the year.

Then there is Lenny. He has a real taste for adventure, and he is always looking for new thrills and excitement, but he's never found enough. At least, not until he came to Ohr Somayach and finally found a lifestyle that satisfied him.

Lenny was once recounting for me the highlights of his expedition through the Okefenokee swamp, a national wildlife refuge filled with alligators and other friendly animals. At one point Lenny described with relish how he was canoeing in one of the many water holes, when he realized he was surrounded by venomous snakes. Not just any venomous snakes. These were the most poisonous snakes to be found in the United States.

I could only stare at him in disbelief. "Lenny, do you mean to say you went to this place voluntarily?"

"You bet, Rabbi! What a rush!"

Maybe so, but apparently not as big a rush as learning Torah.

Is there another yeshivah in the world where the *Purim shpiel* is produced by a former off-Broadway producer, written by a screenwriter, and performed by a cast of former professional actors? And the music — played and written by some of the most fabulously talented musicians and artists I have ever encountered, many of them successful performers in their respective fields. I even got advice from an interior decorator who was studying in the yeshivah. Now I'm just waiting for Calvin Klein to do *teshuvah*. Then maybe I can get myself a new suit.

There's even an Ohio State pool champion on campus should I ever need one.

We call him Jerusalem Fats.

Nowhere Else in the World

There used to be an FFB ("*Frum* From Birth," someone who was born into an observant family) who learned in Ohr Somayach. He wasn't officially part of the yeshivah, but he was always in the *beis midrash*.

I once asked him why, in a city like Jerusalem, which has so many places of Torah, he chose to study in Ohr Somayach. His answer gave me a real charge.

"I can't think of another yeshivah in the world where the guys are so into the learning. They may be wearing headbands, sandals, and occasionally cutoffs, but they're all there because they want to be, and it shows in their learning."

The War Hero

In addition to the high scholastic level at Ohr Somayach, there is a high character quotient as well; you never know who you are going to meet.

Bennett Goldberg was a former U.S. Marine and a real character. One day after *shiur* he said to me, "Hey, Rabbi, wanna see something?" and proceeded to bend his rather prominent nose into every conceivable shape. "See that, Rabbi? There's no cartilage in my nose. It was taken out in the army when my nose was broken."

"Really? How did your nose get broken? Was it in the line of duty?"

"Well, not exactly. You see, when I joined the army, my father gave me two rules to live by: never volunteer, and never say no. My first day at the recruiting center I had just signed up when the sergeant came over to me and said, 'Hey, Goldberg, grab that mop and mop the floor.'

"I was still in my civvies, so I didn't think my dad's rules applied yet. I smiled sweetly and said, 'Sorry, Sarge, I don't think so.' The sergeant, a little guy, smiled back just as sweetly, and said, 'All right, Goldberg, no problem.' I smirked and thought, *No big deal. This army ain't so tough after all.*

"Later, after I had changed into my uniform, I felt a tap on the shoulder. 'You Goldberg? Sarge's office.' Still feeling pretty cocky, I strolled into the office, whereupon the pleasant little sergeant, along with two corporals, proceeded to beat me up so bad that I spent a week in the hospital, where the doctor removed all the cartilage from my nose. Ever since then, Rabbi, I can turn up my nose at anything."

Bennett's moral was, when Dad gives you advice, listen. The Torah advocates listening to parents, and so does common sense.

I always tell this to the boys when they start searching for a wife — the process called "going on *shidduchim*." Even if your parents are not observant, and you don't think they know what you need, when you come home with a young lady and they don't think you should marry her, you don't have to listen to them outright, but you certainly shouldn't dismiss their advice out of hand. No one knows you like your parents, and no one cares about you like they do.

Don't Judge a Buck by Its Cover

Ken "Bucky" Blaustein looked and talked like central casting's idea of a drifter, the mysterious loner who saves the day in every Western ever filmed.

Tall and lanky, with sandy hair and a drawl, all Bucky needed was a pair of six-shooters and a horse, and he could have played Shane. In fact, like the classic drifter, he didn't have very much family, just an elderly father and a sister who lived, to quote him, "somewhere back East."

Prior to his arrival at Ohr Somayach, Bucky had been in London working at a job he didn't really like when he decided he wanted to visit Israel. A genuine drifter would have just lit right out, but Bucky, though he didn't need the money and against his friends' urgings, decided to remain in London until the job was done. He stayed the last three weeks, picked up his meager paycheck, and came to Israel to wander.

Bucky's personality seemed so laid-back, so carefree, that when he told me this story, I just had to ask, "Bucky, tell me something. Why didn't you just quit the job and leave?"

"Hey, Rabbi, you know, I made a commitment. I told the guy I was gonna finish the job. I don't quit. I just don't work that way."

This unexpected innate sense of responsibility eventually led Bucky to a full religious commitment.

Poor Richie's Almanacs

I was crushed. It was one of those moments when one must admit the truth to himself — and it hurt.

You see, Richie Shaefer and I were talking sports today, and I found out what it means to really know sports. I have always been considered something of a maven in sports, with a broad knowledge of many minor statistics, gleaned in my youth and stuck in my brain since then. This kid was half my age, and he knew everything — home runs, ERA's, RBI's, base runners left stranded, all the fine print. He even knew the players from my era better than I did. I felt like what a small-time club musician must feel when he meets a true musical genius.

But there was a lesson to be learned from all this.

I asked Richie how he got to be so good.

He said, "When I was five or six, my parents started buying me sports almanacs and statistics books. I memorized them all." He paused a moment and added wistfully, "I wish they had bought me a *Chumash* or a *Mishnah*."

Don't we all?

One Student in Ohr Somayach Is Worth How Many Cows?

You may have heard of Yitz Greenbaum, one of the early Israeli Zionist leaders and a man notorious for his antipathy toward Torah and religious Jews. He is famed for his statement, "One cow in Palestine is worth more than a million religious Jews in Europe."

Well, bearing that in mind, read the following story told to me by a rebbe of mine.

One afternoon my rebbe was busy with various tasks, overseeing the sundry details of running a large yeshivah, when someone came running up to him and said, "Rebbe, you've got to come to the conference room right now. We're interviewing a potential student for the yeshivah."

My rebbe, not grasping the uniqueness of this particular interview, said, "Look, I'm kind of busy right now. Maybe someone else can do the interview."

"But, Rebbe, you don't understand. This is not just any student. This is Yitz Greenbaum's grandson!"

"Really?" he exclaimed. "This I've got to see. Yitz Greenbaum's grandson on his way to becoming a religious Jew! To witness how Hashem has brought it all full circle, that is truly a miracle!" He immediately dropped what he was doing and went to meet the young man.

Another descendant of a distinguished politician of Greenbaum's era also came to learn in a famous yeshivah in Eretz Yisrael. This boy's grandfather was a brilliant Marxist theorist and revolutionary, one of the most powerful people in the world, a leader in a country devoted to eliminating religion completely. The country: Russia. The politician: Lev

Davidovitch Bronstein, otherwise known as Leon Trotsky, confidant of Lenin and creator of the Russian Red Army.

Yitz Greenbaum and Leon Trotsky, two brilliant, rebellious Jews, each convinced he had discovered the real solution to the Jewish problem — the abandonment of Torah — in exchange for a utopian political system.

Now they and their movements have crumbled in the dust, while the Torah they tried to eradicate is not only relevant and flourishing, but has become the province of their very own children.

"*Mah gadlu ma'asecha Hashem* — How great are Your works, Hashem!"

A Reverse Invitation

Tony Shabbat seemed to be enchanted with yeshivah and learning. He arrived from Texas looking like your typical party animal, but he was actually very bright and loved to learn. He advanced quickly in his learning, and his praying soon became quite intense. This is usually a warning sign, but in Tony's case he seemed balanced, so we didn't discourage his devotion. It was the right call; Tony continued on an upward curve in Torah attainment, while remaining a normal, fun-loving guy.

After a couple of years of study, Tony had become a fine religious Jew and decided to begin looking for a *shidduch*. Unfortunately, for no discernible reason, nothing seemed to work out in that area, which left Tony somewhat depressed. His search went on and on, until finally, still unmarried, he was forced by family circumstances to return home to Texas.

Now if you think Jerusalem is a tough place to find a nice Jewish girl, just try Texas.

I really did not want to see him leave. Tony had no choice; he had to go home. When he left, I wished him all the best and told him that I hoped we'd be seeing him again soon, with a family.

Sometime later another Texan arrived in yeshivah. I inquired if he knew Tony and was told, "Sure, I know Tony. In fact, he had a big influence on my becoming observant."

"Oh, really? So how is he doing? Did he find a *shidduch* yet?"

In lieu of a reply, I received a sad shake of the head.

"What's wrong? What happened? Is Tony all right?"

"Well, Rabbi, physically he's all right. But spiritually he's not doing too well. Texas isn't the best place for Tony. Once he got back in his old environment, he slowly slipped away from *Yiddishkeit*. Recently he went to work in a discotheque. He no longer wears a yarmulke and is really not observant at all."

I was shocked and saddened. On the one hand, we'd lost a Jewish *neshamah*, certainly for the time being. That was sad enough. But it was more than that.

I liked Tony very much on a personal level. He's a very special young man. He had amassed so much knowledge, such a clear understanding of life's purpose, and had such a firm commitment to Torah and its values, that there was no way he gave it up casually. There was no question that Tony was hurting inside, having been forced by unfortunate circumstances to give up a way of life he truly held dear.

I couldn't help but feel the pain he had to be feeling alone in Texas, knowing he was living a life that contradicted those eternal values, what he truly believed. I was sure that each time he did something that was not congruent with Torah, Tony had to go through his own personal gehinnom.

Tony, you can come back any time you want to. We'll accept you with open arms.

And Who by Fire...

There is a young man currently studying at Ohr Somayach who was formerly a captain in U.S. Army Intelligence. He was brought up in New Jersey in a home that was, in his words, "Egalitarian Reform

Conservative Jewish. In short, anything but Orthodox."

One Friday night he was at our house for the meal, and I asked him what it was that got him, an accomplished "anything-but-Orthodox" Jew, interested in *Yiddishkeit*. He told us a fascinating story, the end of which has not yet been written, since his parents, following in their son's footsteps, are now beginning to discover the beauty of Torah Judaism.

To relate the entire tale would require a whole chapter, but I will share with you the beginning of the story, which is an amazing illustration of the confluence of "happenstance" and the inextinguishable Jewish soul.

Barry was attending a small liberal-arts school in New Jersey, more or less dividing his time between the swim team, classes, and late-night partying. He shared a rather large townhouse with the other members of his fraternity and never experienced any discrimination, though there was only one other Jewish member.

One Friday night, during an especially raucous party, Barry found himself lying on the floor of the living room, in front of the roaring fire, hovering somewhere between inebriation and unconsciousness. Through the mists he heard his frat brother saying, "Yo, Barry, look at this. Look what I found."

Barry opened his bleary eyes and made out his friend Doug holding out a bunch of rolled-up little papers, some with black writing on the outside and partially torn. From some dim memory he recognized them as mezuzos, and he said, "Where'd you get those, Doug?"

"I found 'em hanging on the doorposts, man. I ripped 'em all off. You know what they are?"

"Yeah, man. They're a Jewish religious thing. You shouldn't have ripped them off. That's not cool."

"Oh. Right. You want them, Barry?"

"Yeah, give 'em to me. I'll put them back up."

"You really want them?" teased Doug, holding them out to Barry, but just out of his reach.

"Yeah, give 'em to me, man. Stop playing around."

"Well, if you want them, take them. Here!" And Doug tossed the mezuzos straight into the fire.

Barry looked on in horror. There was nothing he could do. The mezuzos were consumed by the fire in an instant.

Although he had never even noticed that the house had mezuzos on the doors, and there was no logical reason that their destruction should bother him, he felt violated, as though he had been attacked in a very personal way.

Still not entirely sure why, he picked himself up off the floor and made his way to the door crying. He walked out the door and kept walking for a very long time.

Something hidden deep inside him had been touched, and he wanted to know what it was. If he could feel so strongly about an obscure religious item, then he had better find out what this item represented and why it was able to exert such an influence on him, a secular, "anything-but-Orthodox" Jew.

— E. M.

True Fear

Mason Levy had had a very sad childhood. His father had been killed when he was younger, and his mother was physically unwell.

One evening some boys came looking for me. "Rabbi, Mason's not doing too good."

I went to his dorm and found him sitting on the steps, crying like a baby.

"Rabbi, my mom's not well. I don't want her to die… I'll be alone."

I sat with him for two hours, trying to keep from crying myself.

They didn't tell me about this when I took the job.

Ted and Moses

Ted Lichtman's story is a classic. After college he traveled through several Arab countries. His last stop was Jordan, so when he got there, he really enjoyed himself. One day he went climbing over the Drur Mountains, which overlook Israel. Gazing down at the panoramic view of the east bank of Israel, he remembered something he had once heard in Hebrew school.

He said to himself, *Hey, that's the land even Moses wasn't allowed to enter. I've got to check it out.*

You can probably guess the end of the story. Ted somehow found his way to Ohr Somayach and got hooked on Moses.

Today he learns in *kollel* and is the proud father of a beautiful little boy.

My Rabbi Is Bigger than Yours

Terry Goodman is a sweet guy, but he was not blessed with great social or intellectual skills. He wasn't having much success at Ohr Somayach, since the learning level is rather advanced, and I had wondered whether he was feeling satisfied and accomplished.

I was pleasantly surprised to overhear him tell a friend one day, "You know, I really love this place. And you know why? Everyone's always so friendly. If I pass anyone, even the biggest rabbi, he says hello. They all make you feel like you belong. Here, watch this!"

Proceeding to anoint me a "biggest rabbi," Terry walked over to me and said, "Hi, Rabbi."

What could I do? I gave him a big smile. "Hi, Terry, how's it going?"

He turned to his friend and said, "See what I mean?"

One never knows how a small action on the giving end can reap big effects on the receiving end.

L'Chaim!

Robert Jackson sent me this thank you card after I performed his son's *pidyon haben*:

> Dear Rabbi Kaplan,
> Thank you for the spirited redemption ceremony. I definitely felt something... I don't know if it was my *neshamah* being elevated, the great guests who were there...or the wine.

Napoleonic Syndrome

There is a fascinating statement in the Talmud that has always puzzled me. The Talmud says that Pharaoh was one cubit tall, about twenty-one inches, and Nevuchadnetzar was the size of a jug.

That's small. That's P. T. Barnum size.

It's mind-boggling to think that two great world rulers were the size of Tom Thumb. It is hard to imagine that two such physically small people could really control legions of hardened warriors and run the most powerful countries of their time.

But beyond that, I've always wondered, what is the significance of this statement? Why do the Sages find it necessary to tell us about this phenomenon? What can we learn from the fact that these people were so small in stature?

There is a discussion in the commentaries as to whether the Sages were being literal in this instance or allegorical. If it is allegory, the question is even stronger.

The Sages use allegory to teach us lessons, often moral lessons. What lesson are we to learn from their descriptive of Pharaoh and his descendant?

Something I heard from a former Hollywood bigwig sheds some light on the subject.

Jerry, an extraordinarily talented actor and writer, was a collaborator on one of the most successful theater hits of all time. He was a very successful music producer as well, having gone quadruple platinum with an album by the rock group Foreigner.

In fact, "foreigner" might have been an apt description of Jerry at that time in his life — foreigner to his people, foreigner to religion, foreigner to anything spiritual.

Today Jerry, now known as Yerucham, still has an audience of thousands, but they are reading and studying the words of Torah he so elegantly formulates each week for a well-known electronic Torah newsletter.

When Jerry got married, he spoke at one of his *sheva berachos*, and this is what he said:

"I was acquainted with many of the biggest names in Hollywood and show business, and you know, for all their wealth and power, they were really very small people. In fact, the better one got to know them, the smaller they seemed.

"They projected a pompous public persona, but when you knew them, you saw that they were really about two feet tall."

That's when it hit me. This is what the Sages are telling us with regard to Pharaoh.

Don't be impressed by the position a person holds or by his seeming power and glory, they are saying. It's what is inside the person that matters. If all a person seeks is his own aggrandizement and pleasure, he really is only two feet tall.

My Son...the Doctor?

A lot of the guys who come to yeshivah find themselves undergoing great changes in their lives. They may realize that what they thought they wanted to spend their lives doing has changed with exposure to Torah and *Yiddishkeit*. Occasionally career plans will even be altered. But one guy's experience was unique. This young man was a premed student at a prominent university and had done volunteer work for the NYU emergency room. He just knew he was going to be a doctor.

One summer morning there was a bris in the yeshivah. This young man pushed his way to the front for a good look at the proceedings. Suddenly there was a commotion. People started pushing and yelling, "Give him air! Give him air!" For a moment I thought something had happened to the baby.

But no. It seemed that our intrepid sawbones had passed out at the sight of blood.

Well, maybe he'll become *frum* and try his hand at being a rabbi. One can usually avoid blood in that line of work.

The REAL United Nations

The Torah tells us that at the proper time God will gather in all the exiled Jews from all over the world and return them to their proper place in the Land of Israel.

Every day in our prayers, we mention this promise and ask God to please do this soon so that all of the Jewish nation will once again be together, serving their Creator in their rightful homeland.

In the meantime, there is Ohr Somayach. At any time, a visitor can hear up to five different languages in the various study halls scattered throughout the building.

There's been a large Spanish contingent, an even larger Russian group, and a healthy mix of Israelis, Americans, French, and South African boys.

Just the other day I was sitting in the main *beis midrash*, and I identified seven distinct languages — English, Hungarian, Afrikaans, French, Yiddish, Hebrew, and Spanish. There was even a group speaking that American dialect known as "jive."

Seven different languages, to be sure — but there is one thing that unites all these disparate conversationalists. It is the subject of their discussion, the eternal language of Torah.

Kiruv Questions

KIRUV QUESTIONS

> The peaks of human wisdom may be infinite, but bottomless, too, is the pit of ignorance.
>
> — Anonymous

There are numerous issues with which I have been confronted as I have made my way through the world of *kiruv* and teaching. Some of these issues are philosophical, such as "Why are we here?" or "What is the purpose of life?" Some are science-based questions, concerning how science corresponds with Torah in areas like archaeology and astronomy.

And sometimes the question is not philosophical at all, but is an expression of simple wonder: Why do you study so much? What is so meaningful about Judaism? Why do you have all these archaic rules?

For the past few years, I've had the privilege of teaching in the highly acclaimed Ohr Lagolah program, Ohr Somayach's leadership training institute in Jerusalem. A major goal of Ohr Lagolah is preparing young men for careers in Torah outreach. We try to give them tools with which to utilize their Torah knowledge, personalities, and talents in presenting Torah to the world at large. Ohr Lagolah's training program includes practical rabbinical training, guidelines for preparing classes and lectures, and many other useful skills, including hands-on speaking engagements and lectures.

One of the most important messages I try to impart is that every yeshivah boy, and girl for that matter, is far better prepared for the task of *kiruv* than they realize. The sheer amount of knowledge and depth of analytical training to which they have been exposed in yeshivah affords them a tremendous advantage in the world of *kiruv*.

I might begin my opening lesson with the above quote. It seems to me that it describes perfectly the world in which we live today. Despite our so-called progress and the inundation of marvelous technology in our everyday lives, I don't think this knowledge has made us any wiser, only more data-filled. No one has time to ponder anymore, to think things through slowly; if something can't be said in five seconds or less, it doesn't get said. Or if it gets said, no one listens, since the audience has already changed channels.

A study done at a prestigious Ivy League university showed that the average student does not have an attention span of more than eight minutes at a time. Why that precise time limit? The researchers concluded that eight minutes was the interval between television commercials. People are able to concentrate only for the duration of their favorite TV show.

What this means is that the world may be getting faster, but it's not getting any smarter. Instead of acquiring a new piece of information, and spending some time thinking it over and analyzing it, we flit from one stimulus to the next without properly absorbing the first one.

The Internet is a perfect example of this phenomenon; it's full of most of the world's accumulated information, available within minutes, but no one seems to be getting any wiser from it. If anything, the reverse may be true; instead of real research, the Internet is used for shortcuts and mindless chats.

In case you were wondering, I should tell you that there is a point to this rant. I'm not just writing it to get one of my pet peeves off my mind.

We often think that despite all our Jewish knowledge and scholarship, and all the learning we've done through our years in yeshivah, we're not really prepared to go out there and actually bring people to *Yiddishkeit*.

We think, *What if they ask us this question? What if he says this? What if they say that? I may not know what to answer.* Because of this doubt, we avoid opportunities where we can positively influence other Jews. Our hesitation can prevent us from having real contact with nonobservant Jews and keep us from helping them see the beauty and truth of *Yiddishkeit*.

Well, I'm here to tell you, you are much better prepared than you think, and the world is much less prepared than you may think!

While it's true that occasionally you might meet a tough customer, and a little training never hurts, as even Chazal say, "*Da mah shetashiv* — You must know how to respond," lack of formal preparation should not be seen as a deterrent to getting involved. For one thing, we often don't realize how much knowledge and understanding we have accumulated in a lifetime of being *frum*; until we have to express it, we don't realize it's there. There is no other society in which even the layman spends so much time studying and thinking about his religion and his beliefs. Like the prophet says, "If you are small in your own eyes, you are yet fit to be a leader of Israel."

Perhaps even more important, the secular world for the most part gives so little attention to spiritual matters that it is not even prepared for simple logical deconstruction of its belief systems. Like I said, most people don't like to think any more than necessary, certainly not about deep spiritual matters that require more than five minutes to resolve.

So fear not — they haven't been working on ways to disprove the Torah. Most likely, they haven't even thought about it at all. And this is true not only of the average citizen, but even of the so-called rabbis.

So remember, you don't have to be the *gadol hador* to be *mekarev* people. You just have to be you.

The Educated Consumer

As I've mentioned, there are many different methods of *kiruv*, all of which, depending on the people involved, can be very effective. To maximize one's effectiveness, however, it is worth identifying an approach that works for you and can be used consistently with as many people as possible.

My colleagues at Ohr Somayach and I have found the most effective approach to *kiruv* to be somewhat akin to the famous Syms slogan: "An educated consumer is our best customer."

When a young man comes in off the street, not quite sure what he may be looking for, we don't start drowning him in Orthodox theology and all of the lofty concepts of Judaism. Those things are all fine, and will be presented in time, but our first aim is to get to the actual studying as quickly as possible.

We introduce the newcomer to some basic essentials of Judaism and then immediately begin teaching him how to read Hebrew. We want to introduce him to the Torah, to the heart and mind of Judaism. We try to educate him in the beauty of the Gemara, the Talmud, as soon as possible. Once a student has begun Torah study, everything else will follow in due course. I can't explain it logically, but experience has shown that Gemara learning is the quickest method of turning idle curiosity into real commitment.

Our approach is to give a student an introductory Gemara *shiur* and let him enjoy the logic of the Gemara, even if he can't yet read the text. In most cases, the student will get interested just by the logic and organization of the discussion.

Once a newcomer has an appreciation and an interest in the subject matter, the next step is to help him learn to read the text by himself. This can take anywhere from a month to three months, depending on a student's previous experience and his inherent ability to grasp a new language.

When the student can actually read the Talmud in the original and follow the reasoning on his own, he can take the learning to a whole new level. He starts to delve into the text and the commentaries to the point where he can really enjoy the *sugya*, the give-and-take and subtle nuances of a Talmudic discussion. From that point, it's a matter of working and refining his skills. The commitment to Judaism usually follows of its own accord.

As for the effect Gemara has on the students, I can't do better than to let the students speak for themselves. I once took a survey, asking students, most of whom were already observant, what role Gemara study played in their becoming observant. The following are some of their responses:

— "Gemara had a huge role in my commitment to Judaism. I even transferred schools to continue learning Gemara while I got my degree."

— "Gemara learning was so logical and perfect. It just made me feel good."

— "The logic and integrity of the Talmud made me see the validity of the Torah. I realized that these arguments couldn't be made up by man."

— "A *huge role*. It's the main reason I became *frum*. All that philosophy is fine, but it doesn't make you *frum*."

— "It helped me distinguish between my emotions and my intellect."

— "Before I started learning Gemara, things were blurry, like seeing underwater, but now things are as clear as if I am looking at them under a microscope."

— "It's the glue that kept me together through the early stages."

— "It's central to my commitment. It showed me that for something to get past those rabbis it had to be true."

— "It's the key to the doorway of international *Yiddishkeit*." (I'm not really sure what that means, but it seems like a nice turn of phrase.)

And my personal favorite, from a student not yet fully committed:

— "I'm afraid to continue learning Gemara because it's having an effect on me. I think it's going to make me *frum*."

Students often ask me why we are studying Talmudic subjects that have no application in day-to-day living, such as oxen goring cows, the sacrificial laws of the Temple, or the laws of the *Sanhedrin*, which are not in effect today.

My explanation is that there are plenty of practical applications because these laws form the legal precedents from which our contemporary laws are drawn. Also, these laws, though we do not practice them, do have an effect on our lives, and they are relevant today in a metaphysical way. For example, the Talmud says that although we cannot bring offerings today, anyone who learns about the Temple service is considered to have brought an actual offering. And this is true with regard to all Talmudic subjects, that one who studies them is considered to have actually fulfilled their laws. This is because the Torah is not just one aspect of the world we live in, but its very blueprint, and, as such, its study is considered a more than adequate replacement for the physical reality. That is the logical explanation.

But it is not the logical explanation that I need as much as the super-logical results I see for myself. The changes in the boys' behavior, in their personal relationships, and in their religious commitment are all the validation I need of the Torah's inherent power to change a person.

I can't point to a specific law in the Torah and say, "Look, if you study that page, you will become a better person." But I can say that through the study of Gemara, even the so-called illogical laws of the Torah, one can see a tremendous change in the person doing the studying. The very act of studying has an effect on one's life in all its aspects.

An Eternal Connection

Fred Davidson was a very bright fellow on leave from a prestigious law firm. For the first three weeks that Fred attended the Gemara *shiur* he was befuddled. He just couldn't comprehend the Gemara's logic. Every time we posed a question in class and suggested the answer, Fred's answer was always the opposite. He had a perpetually puzzled expression on his face. He tried hard, but it was tough for him to keep up with the *shiur*.

After about three weeks, he suddenly got the knack of it, and then he truly became interested. He turned Gemara learning into his personal crusade and was very successful at it. Fred left the yeshivah a few years ago, but to this day we have kept in touch. And despite leading very different lives, Fred as a successful lawyer, myself as a black-hatted Orthodox rebbe, the glue that keeps us together is our common love for learning.

That is one of the greatest things about giving a Gemara *shiur* and about studying Gemara one-on-one with a *chavrusa*: the bond that is formed almost effortlessly, a Torah connection that lasts long beyond the moment.

Kenny Seltzer came to the yeshivah and became a regular student in my Gemara *shiur*. He made it very clear to me that he planned on being in yeshivah for only a few months and then he was going on to a Conservative seminary. Kenny was a bright guy, and we enjoyed studying Gemara together.

He did indeed go to the Conservative seminary eventually, but thanks to our studying together, we have stayed in touch until this day. Whenever he visits Israel, he comes to the yeshivah to study.

The Cultural Divide

There are certain things one has to get used to when learning with freshly minted *ba'alei teshuvah*. Cultural things.

Sometimes, when teaching Gemara, one can spark off certain reactions, reactions you probably wouldn't get in, say, Ponovezh Yeshivah. A student might make a comment about the Gemara topic, and you'll hear, "Yo, Shuck, that was pretty clever." And everyone gets up and high-fives everyone else in the room.

Once Arthur stood up and said, "Rabbi, no offense, but I don't agree with that guy Papa and his friends. I agree with Nachman."

"Uh, Arthur, it's Rav Papa and Rav Nachman to you."

"Yeah, well, I don't agree with those guys."

"Arthur, Rav Papa and Rav Nachman are not 'guys.' They were able to bring dead people back to life. Any Rabbi mentioned in the Talmud could bring the dead to life. Please treat them with due respect."

"Oh, all right, but whatever the title, I don't agree with them."

These are moments that take some getting used to, but on the way the students are introduced to the beauty, depth, and essence of Torah learning.

Another young man remarked in *shiur*, "Hey, *Tosafos* is really bugging out on *Rashi!*"

Although it's true that such terminology is generally not used in Brisk or Mir, the boy *was* learning *Tosafos*.

Chillin' Like Dylan

Part of the difficulty in teaching Gemara to beginners occurs when the Gemara or the commentaries make use of a word that has multiple meanings or is used in a colloquial manner rather than its normal fashion.

It can be hard for beginners to assimilate the idea that their hard-earned understanding of a word has suddenly changed to mean something else.

A breakthrough took place one day when Nachy Jacobs put his head down in the middle of *shiur*.

"Nachy, are you feeling all right?"

"Yeah, Rabbi, I'm fine. I'm just mad tired."

"I'm sorry to hear that. What are you mad about?"

"No, I'm not mad. I'm tired."

"I thought you said you were mad."

"I said I was mad tired."

"Huh?"

Well, it turns out that *mad*, besides for meaning "angry," can also mean "very," as in "mad hungry" or "mad happy," or even, as Nachy once told me, referring to a fast water-park slide, "mad good."

Although I've never actually heard anyone say it, I suppose one could also be "mad mad." I just hope I'm not there to see it.

It was, as are many aspects of my job, an education for me. It was also helpful, since I used my newfound knowledge to illustrate to the students that language is constantly changing, and a word that means one thing in one locale can have an entirely different connotation elsewhere or in a different time period. This is of tremendous benefit in clarifying the myriad usages of words in the Gemara and the analyses of the commentaries in this regard.

I have since discovered that "buggin' out" is bad and "chillin' out" is good, especially "chillin' like Dylan." *Good* and *bad* are themselves somewhat ambiguous, however; in certain cases *bad* can mean "good," as in "That shwarma was really bad, man." This means the shwarma was especially tasty and nutritious.

So I guess Nachy falling asleep in the middle of *shiur* turned out to be something very good — or, as one might say, "mad bad."

Harder than Med School

The question of the proper methodology for teaching Gemara is far beyond the scope of this book. There is, in fact, no one proper methodology. But a few general points do stand out and bear mentioning.

First, I've found that preparing a Gemara *shiur* for beginners is a real challenge. It requires a lot more than just reading and translating. I must study the *gemara* and know it well, even better than if I were teaching it to experienced learners. With experienced guys, there are certain things one can assume they know, and they won't require detailed explanation, but with beginners, it's all new, and I'd better understand it perfectly if I'm going to be able to teach it to them.

Also, they may be Gemara-text novices, but when I get into a logical discussion, I find that these people can think, and they can ask some very tough questions.

When I ask a young man which school he comes from, and he names a high-level place like Harvard or Cambridge, I get nervous. They may not be experienced Talmud scholars, but they all have one common denominator: they're smart. And in a class full of smart people, if what I am saying isn't tight and logical, they'll pick up on it and make me look bad, which, like most people, is something I don't particularly enjoy.

What I do enjoy, however, is watching accomplished professionals, such as doctors and lawyers, sweating over a relatively simple piece of Gemara, and I'm thinking to myself, *They didn't prepare you for this in law school, did they?*

Of course, I'd be sweating just as hard over a law book or a medical journal. That's why I steer clear of them.

What a Beginner Is Looking At

I often try to demonstrate to budding *kiruv* workers what it is like for a *ba'al teshuvah* or other beginners to start learning Gemara at an advanced age. For someone steeped in lifelong Jewish scholarship, it's hard to fully appreciate the difficulty of this enterprise. But it is important to understand the enormity of the task for reasons both pedagogic and empathetic.

I start by reminding my listeners that these beginners barely read Hebrew, much less Aramaic. They are tackling less-than-modern case histories, written in a style that eschews vowels and punctuation, often resorts to contractions and acronyms, and, just to make things even more confusing, uses idioms whose meanings are miles removed from their literal translation (such as *af al pi*, which means "nose on mouth," but in Gemara language means "even though"). Oh yes, and every now and then, the Gemara does throw in a vowel or a little punctuation, which tends to throw the beginner even further off course.

Despite this introduction, it is still difficult for an outsider to grasp the magnitude of the undertaking, so I distribute a visual aid to illustrate exactly what a *ba'al teshuvah* is looking at. This helps enormously in giving these future teachers a clearer idea of the challenge.

I hand out a paper with the script below and ask the students, experienced Gemara scholars all, to decipher and explain the words on the page. It is really amusing to watch as they confidently start reading and then, usually three lines in, hit the wall.

Bear in mind that the following is in a well-known chapter of Gemara. The students are experienced, and they are reading in a language with which they are familiar, English.

> a gy sd to his fllw wht ar yu dng on ths lnd frm plni i bght it and cnsmd it lng engh to mk a chzka hs a thf bt i hv wtnss tht yu advsd me to prchs it frm hm i sd th scnd is esr thn th frst sd rvu he hs tld hm th lw lke whm admn as ws tght in a mshn one tht cntnos on a fld and is sgnd on it as a wtnss admn sys the scnd is esr the frst is dffclt and thch"s hs lst hs rghta a"t rbnn thr he dd an actn hr its spch pple wll smtms sy.

By the time the guys have spent five minutes on this, they have a vastly increased appreciation for what a *ba'al teshuvah* is dealing with as he embarks on the study of Gemara.

Oh, and if you want to know what you were just reading, just look up *masechta...daf...*

It's all right there, in black and white.

(For the source, see the end of this chapter.)

Some Brains Could USE a Good Washing

As I was leaving yeshivah for the day, I noticed an older man, perhaps in his mid-sixties, standing uncertainly by the steps leading up to the entrance. I asked if I could help him, and he said he was looking for a certain young man. I told him with a smile, "I'm sorry, I don't know where he is right now, but you are more than welcome to join a class while you wait for him." I expected him to jokingly refuse, but I sure didn't foresee what was coming.

"No, I'm not interested in any of your classes. I know what you do to these boys. I know the type of brainwashing you put them through."

This I needed at the end of a full day. I felt like walking away. Of course, I didn't.

"Brainwashing? You mean that presenting adults with ideas is called brainwashing? To open their undernourished minds to the beauty of Torah and tradition is brainwashing? That's not brainwashing!

"They are free to leave anytime they want. No one forces them to stay here. We supply them with a balanced diet. That's not brainwashing. We encourage them to ask questions. That's not brainwashing.

"How about the universities? Are they also brainwashing when they present their students with unfamiliar information?"

"No, I know all about it. I know what you do to these boys."

He didn't want to hear the truth. I'm not sure what his background was, but it was obvious that if anyone was brainwashed, it was he.

The brainwashing canard is one of the most common, and most fallacious, accusations leveled at yeshivos. I often hear from beginner students, "Aren't you brainwashing us?" or from unknowledgeable outsiders, "Aren't you brainwashing them?" It's so ludicrous as to be almost pointless to refute.

Brainwashing by definition entails restriction of movement and diet, force-feeding of ideas, and not allowing for challenges, none of which take place at any yeshivah. Presentation of ideas, whether true or false, the free and open exchange of information, does not constitute brainwashing.

When I'm faced with this line of questioning, I make the inquisitor define *brainwashing*. Once the mists are cleared away, the honest questioner will realize that he is just spouting a cliché with no basis in reality.

A Sacrificial Beef

Another thing I've learned is that one should never apologize for his belief in the Torah. There is nothing wrong with trying to explain Torah and Jewish tradition from a logical, commonsense point of view, but one should always remember that the ultimate arbiter of logic is the holy Torah, and the fact that we don't see the reason for a law doesn't negate its truth.

One day we were discussing the sacrificial service in the Temple when a hand went up, not so much to request permission to speak as to herald a pronouncement.

"I think it's wrong to kill animals."

"Joey, I agree with you. It is wrong to kill animals unnecessarily."

"What do you mean, you agree that it's wrong? You're telling us all about this sacrificial service. Let me ask you something, Rabbi. You're a *kohen*, aren't you? If the third Beis HaMikdash were built, wouldn't you be sacrificing animals in the Beis HaMikdash?"

"Yes, I certainly hope so."

"But you just told me it's wrong to kill animals."

"It is."

"Rabbi, I don't understand."

"To kill animals for no reason is wrong. To sacrifice in the Beis HaMikdash, in order to serve God, is not wrong."

"Why isn't it wrong? What are you accomplishing with the sacrifice of an animal?" He was getting hot under the collar.

"Joey, do you wear a belt?"

"Yeah."

"What's it made out of?"

"Leather. Look, Rabbi, I know what you're getting at, but there's a big difference. The belt holds my pants up."

"No, there is no difference at all. You think a belt is a necessity, and that permits you to kill an animal for its hide. But it's not really that important. You could wear suspenders instead of a belt.

"And how about your shoes? Those are leather Nikes. You have no objections to killing animals for these reasons. Isn't that correct, Joey?"

"Come on, there's a big difference between that and animal sacrifices. Sacrifices are pointless!"

"Well, that's what you say. We understand that animals were given to humans to fulfill any human need. We don't kill or harm animals unnecessarily. Even hunting for sport provokes a discussion in the halachah as to whether sport is a legitimate reason to harm animals.

But if something is necessary, we have no problem with using animals for their intended purpose.

"We think sacrifice is a legitimate human need. The Torah commands us to bring certain sacrifices and allows us to bring other voluntary ones, and that is at least as legitimate a need as a leather motorcycle jacket.

"You may not think sacrifices are all that important, but then again, you're not looking at it from the Torah perspective.

"In fact, Joey, on a deeper level, it is a benefit to the animal to be brought as a sacrifice. That way it is used in the service of God instead of being used for something mundane, like someone's backyard barbecue."

Mr. Know-It-All

Sometimes you have to be creative to get your point across.

Steve Chait loved to talk. Whatever the subject, Steve knew it better and could do it better. He was such a shmoozer he even practiced his talking during class. Despite this slight failing, Steve was a nice boy who was really coming along in his learning, and I was hopeful that with more time in yeshivah, Steve would really blossom.

Now if there was any subject Steve especially liked to talk about, it was sports. Steve knew everything about everything, but when it came to sports, he saw himself as an absolute authority.

I owe a debt of gratitude to Michael Jordan and the Chicago Bulls. Being from Chicago, I can easily put down any other city in basketball braggadocio, especially New York, where Steve was from.

One day, after a particularly annoying filibuster from Steve on the subject of the Big Apple and its basketball team, I lost my patience, and I challenged Steve to a shootout on the basketball court.

The stakes: another year in yeshivah for Steve.

Well, to Steve's undying amazement, he lost — badly. He was humbled, beaten by an older rabbi with thick glasses.

It was, quite literally, the first time I had ever seen him speechless. Not only that, the bet was paid off. Well, sort of. Steve left and I spent another year in yeshivah.

I tried it again a few years later with Terry Reiss, but, although close, I couldn't quite beat him. Bear in mind, though, Terry is a fellow Chicagoan, so losing to him was understandable.

The Truth Is, I Just Gotta Get Married

Clive Markowitz was an easygoing, friendly South African with a deep intellectual curiosity. He took an immediate liking to Gemara learning due to its analytical nature and unceasing inquiry into the truth. Clive also adapted well to the yeshivah atmosphere and quickly became a popular figure around campus.

He was a model student in all ways but one. He claimed to be a committed atheist and would not adopt any of the customs or laws of Judaism. Of course, out of respect for the yeshivah he wouldn't desecrate Shabbos or do any other *aveiros* publicly. He simply did his own thing and indulged in the intellectual pursuits we offered.

When I felt the time was right, I invited Clive into the office for a chat. Having been told that he was an atheist, and knowing his penchant for rational inquiry, I fully anticipated an engaging debate on the existence of God and similar topics.

"So, Clive, what do you think of Gemara?"

Big smile. "Yeah, I really like it. Very stimulating intellectually."

"How about yeshivah in general?"

"Amazing. I've met some remarkable people. I couldn't be happier."

"So tell me, Clive, do you have any specific questions about Judaism. Is anything bothering you?"

Again the friendly smile. "No, not really."

"Are you sure. Nothing at all? I'll be glad to discuss it with you."

"No, I'm fine, Rabbi. It's all good."

"Really!? I mean, great! Uh, well, have a good day."

This exchange repeated itself several times over the succeeding months as Clive made great strides in his scholastic attainments and none at all in his religious commitment.

With smug self-confidence, which interestingly did not detract at all from his pleasant personality, he continued to claim that he simply wasn't convinced of the truth of Judaism. To be honest, he didn't give Judaism a real chance. He continued to forestall any attempt at a serious theological discussion. But it didn't bother him. He still liked to learn; he just didn't daven or perform any mitzvos.

Clive turned out to be unusually steadfast in his lack of belief. He remained in the yeshivah for quite some time, learning, behaving well, but not moving an iota toward Torah practice. When he left, it was with smiles all around, but with a deeply felt sense of disappointment that we could not get him to make a real change in his lifestyle. There was also a sense of frustration at his deliberate obtuseness and muleheaded refusal to examine the evidence properly.

About three months after Clive left yeshivah, I ran into his cousin and asked how Clive was doing.

"Oh, very well. He met a young lady and he's hoping to marry her. Actually, Rabbi, she's quite religious, and she is insisting on a religious commitment from him or no dice."

Well, believe it or not, Clive didn't let the "truth of Judaism" stand in his way any longer. He made the commitment, and they got married.

Sometimes all the arguments and theology in the world don't measure up to a good old-fashioned slice of self-interest. In other words, he wanted the dice.

Another Version of the Truth

I read a great story in the paper, one that perfectly illustrates today's attitude toward truth, or the lack thereof. A certain famous NFL wide receiver stayed out one night partying and arrived bleary-eyed at the team residence at about seven o'clock the following morning.

When confronted by his irate coach as to his whereabouts the previous night, the fellow protested, "I don't know why you're so upset. I came back at about twelve o'clock last night, and I realized I had lost my key. So instead of waking everyone up, I slept in the hammock in the backyard all night."

The coach studied him carefully. "Are you sure that that's what happened, Freddy?"

"Yes, I am."

"Well, buddy, I hate to tell you this, but I threw out that old hammock over a month ago. So what do you say now?"

"Well, that's my story, and I'm sticking to it."

The point is, of course, it may appear noble to stick to your story, but not when it's been proven to be full of holes.

I know, being involved in *kiruv*, that I've got one thing going for me that no one else can claim. I'm selling a unique commodity: the Truth.

All the fancy philosophies and theories, all the self-assured truths, will eventually crumble before us, because we've got the strongest weapon of all: the eternal, immutable Torah.*

---

* The source of the *gemara* quoted above is *Bava Basra* 30b — but, of course, you knew that, didn't you?

Parents

PARENTS

I wish all my students were like Gary Michaels — easygoing, personable, serious about life, and brilliant. Gary came to Ohr Somayach with a prestigious job waiting for him in Canada's top law firm. He took to Gemara like a fish to water and by the end of the year had made tremendous progress.

Gary wanted to stay for another year. Three obstacles stood in his path: the proffered job; his father, Gary Michaels Sr.; and, most formidably according to Gary, his mother, Mrs. Ella Michaels.

Gary approached me for advice. I suggested that first he seek a deferment from the law firm and only then approach his parents for their acquiescence.

The law firm agreed to hold his job for another year. Like I said, he was brilliant. But his parents were not so accepting of his decision and were very vocal in expressing their disapproval. Since they would soon be coming to Israel to visit Gary, he asked me if I would meet with them and perhaps manage to convince them to support his decision to continue learning.

We scheduled a meeting for eleven o'clock in the yeshivah office, and right on time Gary knocked and ushered in his parents.

I stood up. "Hi, Mr. and Mrs. —"

"Rabbi, my son is brilliant, and I want him to pursue a career that is going to challenge his mind."

Mrs. Michaels was clearly of the school that the best offense is a good offense.

"Mrs. Michaels, please sit down. Let's talk about this."

Loudly, "Rabbi, my son is absolutely brilliant. He has a career opportunity, and I don't want him to lose it."

I could see why Gary's main concern had been his mother. His father was clearly aware of his role as spectator. He hadn't even opened his mouth yet.

"Um, Mrs. Michaels, I believe the law firm is going to hold his job."

"That may be, but what's going to happen is Gary will stay in the yeshivah for another year, and then who knows what will be?"

"Mrs. Michaels, Gary is willing to assure you that after this year he will take the job."

"Rabbi, Gary is absolutely brilliant, and I want him to use his brilliance in the most challenging manner."

"Uh, have you thought of asking Gary which is the greater strain, the studying he did in law school or the Talmud?"

"That's immaterial, Rabbi. I want him to use his mind."

What she really wanted was to be able to tell her friends already that her son was a prestigious lawyer and earning a lot of money. Which is fine. A mother is entitled to her *nachas*. Moreover, we don't advocate irresponsibility and certainly did not discourage Gary from taking the job. But the legal profession could probably survive one more year without Gary, and another year in yeshivah would do him inestimable good.

Happily Gary eventually managed to sway his parents into letting him stay for another year in yeshivah, as long as he promised to take the proffered job the following year.

At the end of the year, with our encouragement, he fulfilled his commitment and became a practicing lawyer while remaining a strongly committed Torah-observant and Torah-studying Jew.

Postscript: After a year as a lawyer, Gary gave it up, citing mental stagnation as the cause, returned to Israel, and today is married and learning in *kollel*.

A "Moderate" Request

Lawrence Charnowicz's parents were more respectful of his newfound interest in Torah study. Lawrence came from Denver, from an upscale family. He had studied to become a lawyer and, upon graduating law school, became observant. This was perfectly all right with his family. They did not object to Lawrence learning or being Orthodox. The only bone of contention was, quite literally, about bones.

Lawrence had committed to keeping kosher, which meant he could no longer eat at his grandmother's house nor could he join his family for dinner at non-kosher restaurants. Since his parents were very fond of restaurants, this had become a real issue.

Lawrence's parents came to speak with me, and his mother said respectfully, "Rabbi, we're all for religion, and we're happy for Larry that he's found it, but we want moderation. Everything in moderation."

"Yes, Mrs. Charnowicz, we also advise moderation. The only question is, where is the starting point after which moderation kicks in?

"In order to call something moderate, one must know what the extremes are. The extremes don't include Buddhism and atheism. They are measured only within the framework of halachah. Once we have identified the extremes within the halachic system, we can then decide what is more or less moderate. Basic kashrus is not open to compromise."

As a general rule, I always encourage strong family ties and good relationships with parents and siblings, not only for religious reasons, such as *shalom* and the requirement to honor one's parents, but also as a practical matter. If there is opposition from home, it becomes much more difficult for a student, particularly at the early stages of return, to accept and commit to a *frum* lifestyle, since he will feel that becoming religious will alienate him from his family and it may not be worth it.

From the parents' perspective, the greatest fear is usually not religion; it is the fear that their well-ordered family will be torn asunder by their child's return to *Yiddishkeit*.

Occasionally a student will have problems in his familial relationships while becoming *frum*, either because he does not know how to accommodate certain religious traditions with his parents' lifestyle or because he may encounter some perceived hostility and he reacts in kind.

One reality, though, has become clear to me over the years. Usually, if there is strain in the family, you will find that the strain existed before the religious commitment, and the student's return to Torah exacerbated an already volatile situation. If the family relationship was healthy beforehand, it will generally remain healthy afterward as well.

Nevertheless, I still try very hard to make sure the boys retain a good relationship with their parents, and I encourage them to bend over backward in order to avoid strife.

Sometimes, though, no matter how hard the *ba'al teshuvah* tries to keep the peace, the very fact that he has become *frum* upsets the delicate family balance and causes hard feelings. In such a case, the family, like it or not, must bend just a little to accommodate their religious relative.

Can't We All Just Get Along?

Larry Abrams was a case in point. Larry is one of the most sensitive young men I've met in my years in the yeshivah. He arrived in Israel as an exceptionally considerate twenty-five-year-old and immediately began asking the teachers how to avoid upsetting his parents and how to help them adjust to his newfound *Yiddishkeit*. Apparently they were somewhat apprehensive about Larry's chosen path. We encouraged him to stay in touch with his parents, to write home often, and to be as accommodating as possible.

I stayed on top of his situation, and to my knowledge Larry implemented all of our suggestions and went out of his way to keep things peaceful. Eventually Larry's father came to Israel to visit his son and made arrangements to meet me during his stay.

He entered the office, barely mumbled hello, and just sat there looking at me. Whereas some parents are belligerent (see Michaels, Gary), Larry's father was clearly in pain.

"Rabbi, my family is being torn apart."

"How is that, Mr. Abrams?"

"Well, there's me, my wife, Larry, and his sister, Tiffany. We all enjoy sports and have always spent the weekends attending various sporting and cultural events. Now that Larry's religious, he refuses to drive with me to the ball games on Saturday, and it's just tearing my family apart. I even offered to have a non-Jewish friend do the driving, but he says he can't even sit in the car on Saturday. And if I want to take him to the opera, he says he can't listen to a woman sing. Is that true? He's not allowed to listen to a woman sing?"

"Well, to the best of my knowledge, it's frowned upon in the halachah. I could look into it to see if there are any leniencies, but it is certainly discouraged. How else is Larry tearing the family apart?"

"Well, he will no longer watch television with me on Saturday afternoons and..."

He continued with the list of Larry's transgressions, which were "tearing the family apart."

Finally I said, "Mr. Abrams, Larry is twenty-five years old. Isn't he allowed to make choices for himself at this age?"

"Sure, he's allowed to make choices, but I'm an American and I believe in freedom of choice, and a religion where he's going to have his wife picked for him" (a very common misconception about Orthodox dating) "and he's told when he can and can't drive his car, and which foods he can and cannot eat goes against my grain."

"Mr. Abrams, I respect your beliefs. I am also an American, and I also believe in freedom. I would just like to know — does your belief in freedom extend to allowing Larry to choose his own lifestyle?"

"Well, he is..." And then he stopped. Mr. Abrams realized he had not been listening to himself. Freedom is a two-way street, and if Larry, a mature young man, wanted to choose his own way of life, then Mr.

Abrams's own ethos of freedom required that he respect that choice.

Having gotten this far, I decided to take the gloves off. I said, "Mr. Abrams, you say Larry is tearing your family apart. Isn't Larry a part of your family? Here you are, expecting Larry to be sensitive to everything the rest of the family wants to do, to all the needs of the rest of the family. Doesn't he have some rights as a family member?

"According to my calculations, Larry represents twenty-five percent of your family. Shouldn't the rest of the family be sensitive to his needs? Shouldn't some effort be made to accommodate and make adjustments for some of his requirements? He's not asking for very much. I know Larry personally. He's bending over backward to accommodate all of you. The only line he draws is that which the Torah requires of every Jew.

"Larry has committed himself to return to his family's real tradition. If you are interested, I will be happy to discuss the Torah with you and your family. You are welcome to come to the yeshivah and attend some classes. It might help you understand what it is that Larry has undertaken, and, I believe, it will help the whole family stay together and be stronger than ever before. But if we only have twenty minutes together here, I must tell you, sir, you have a fine son, and you succeeded in raising a mensch with strong values. Maintaining good family ties is very high on his list of priorities. We encourage that."

Mr. Abrams softened, but only a little. He left the office still somewhat pained at what he saw as his well-ordered world collapsing. I was told later that our conversation had helped to the extent that Mr. Abrams no longer felt there was a deliberate attempt to isolate Larry and to draw him out of the family unit. Just knowing that made it easier for them to deal with their small disagreements.

I never got to discuss Mr. Abrams's misconceptions about *shidduchim*, but perhaps one day Larry will buy this book for his dad, and that should clear it up.

On the other hand, I remember encountering a newly religious young man in California who was on his way to visit his family in Vermont. He told me he had bought himself a frock, a long black rabbinical coat, because he wanted to look "extra religious."

I was not in a position to influence this boy, but I thought to myself, *You're going to alienate people for no reason.* It turned out later out that he was somewhat mentally unbalanced, a condition that led to a quick marriage and an even quicker divorce.

But I have found this confrontational approach to be extremely rare, and it is certainly not one I advocate.

"You Can Even Marry a Goy — Just as Long as She Isn't Religious!"

Some people are so frightened of their child becoming religious that they prefer intermarriage to a religious marriage.

Eddie Jacobson is a person of unusually fine *middos*. From his warm, easygoing manner, one would think he hadn't a care in the world. In truth, he carries an intense ache deep inside, an ache he keeps to himself so as not to burden anyone else.

You see, Eddie comes from a family very far removed from religious observance. So far removed, in fact, that when one of his siblings married out of the Jewish faith, it didn't make a ripple in the family harmony. His parents went to the interfaith wedding, and they get along fine with their gentile in-laws.

But when Eddie, now Elchanan, got married, his parents refused to come to the wedding. They didn't approve of his and his bride's religious observance.

Elchanan now has a child who is two years old, and his parents still haven't met his wife. That is the pain he carries inside.

Practicing What Dad Preached

Of all the parent-children arguments I've heard with regard to staying in yeshivah, the one between Dave Richter and his parents had to be the shortest.

Dave received a scholarship offer from Stanford University, but instead of going to college immediately, he took off a year to study in yeshivah in Israel. After a year of great spiritual achievement, Dave decided he wanted to study some more.

His parents, although Orthodox Jews and supporters of Torah, were very upset. They felt that Dave was a brilliant boy, which he was, and, having earned a full scholarship to a top university, they didn't think his decision was wise.

Dave sat down one night to discuss the issue with his parents. His opening statement, all by itself, ended the discussion.

He said, "Dad and Mom, remember when I was in high school and Dad was a member of the school's Education Committee? How many nights did I come home and you weren't home, when we often didn't see you till the next morning?

"And why was that? It was because you were sacrificing yourselves and your home life for the perpetuation of Jewish values. There were so many times when I wanted to speak with you, but you weren't around because of your work for Torah education.

"We kids respected that and understood its importance. All I want to do is follow the example you set for me."

Dave has been learning in yeshivah ever since, and he has become a distinguished *talmid chacham* and a true source of pride for his parents.

Doing What's Best for Your Kids

Mrs. Berger called me one day. She was a religious woman from a Jerusalem suburb, and she had a serious problem. Her son Yanky was heading off the *derech*, leaving the Orthodox fold, and she didn't know where to turn. He was no longer communicating very much with his parents, and they were concerned about losing him completely.

The reason she was calling me was that the boy had attended some of my classes at the yeshivah, and he told his mother that he would agree to speak with me about his religious issues.

I told Mrs. Berger I would be glad to meet Yanky and asked her for more information. Apparently the boy was pretty far gone, not really keeping anything anymore, only wearing his yarmulke to make his parents happy. Happy in this case being a relative term, of course.

Yanky came to speak to me. I was pleasantly surprised to find him a nice, polite kid, not a hormone-addled teenager looking for trouble. It didn't take long to find the root of the problem.

Yanky's father had been a very successful, high-powered executive in Memphis who had been living out the American dream, when suddenly he became religious and decided to make major life changes. He moved his family to a small house in a very *frum* neighborhood. This by itself would have been bearable, but since both parents were very enthusiastic about *Yiddishkeit*, and in order to keep their children from repeating their own mistakes, they tried to cut out anything fun and impress upon their kids that it's Torah, Torah, Torah, and everything else is a waste of time.

Of course, this was great for Mommy and Daddy, but for Yanky, a normal American teenager, it was anything but great. He hated every minute of it, starting with living in a religious neighborhood and, eventually, anything having to do with *Yiddishkeit*.

It's hard to tag anyone as the villain in such a case. The parents are well-meaning, sincere people who feel they wasted a good chunk of their lives, and they want their kids to avoid their mistakes.

Yanky certainly couldn't be blamed. He was taken from a fun-loving, secular, all-American environment and thrown into a lifestyle he couldn't handle in a city he didn't know.

So no one's to blame, but we've got a messed-up situation.

Parents have to know that what's good for them, and even what's correct in the strictest sense, is not necessarily the optimal approach for raising children, especially if the parents make a lifestyle change in midstream. It's one thing to raise children from infancy with certain values and life goals, even strict ones, and expect them to adhere to those standards. It's another thing entirely to raise a family with one set of values, or lack of values, as the case may be, and then, just when the children are at a vulnerable age, to completely change the rules on them and expect them to adjust without any problems.

Parents who have decided to make a sudden, significant alteration in their lifestyle must be sensitive to the effect this change will have upon their children and must act accordingly. They have to move slowly and make certain their children are progressing along with them. Obviously the biggest *chesed* a parent can do for their child is to provide them with a Torah upbringing and a lifestyle that avoids the pitfalls they encountered. But if the kids have this kindness rammed down their throats by overzealous parents, then it is no kindness at all and can lead to great heartbreak for all concerned.

It is similar to parents who don't give their kids any sweets at all. In shul, at the *kiddush*, those kids are usually the ones who grab everything in sight. They've been deprived of nosh all week, and in shul there's no one to stop them, so it's open season. The parents think they're doing a great thing, raising healthy, cavity-free kids, but the kids are eating plenty of junk anyway and learning how to be sneaks at the same time.

The same is true of *Yiddishkeit* — parents often don't recognize that their kids don't share their enthusiasm and aren't mature enough yet to appreciate the beauty of religion. They only end up making their children feel pressured to do more than they can handle, often with tragic results.

Yiddishkeit has to be fun and enjoyable. If kids sense it as oppressive and imposing, there is a strong chance that they will eventually reject it.

There is a well-known story of a famous *gadol baTorah* whose son remained religious but left the yeshivah world. Many years later this sage said the reason his son did not stay in learning was because instead of singing *zemiros* at the Shabbos table, and making the meal enjoyable and festive, he had been immersed in studying the Rambam.

Yanky's parents were treading the same path; they never took time to have fun with him, but instead constantly harped on his religious obligations, until finally he got fed up. He told me he didn't want to abandon *Yiddishkeit* completely, but he was tired of the externalities and didn't want to keep them just because of pressure.

I went to visit his parents at their home, and I was shocked at the austerity, even the poverty, reflected in the apartment. These were affluent people. On the one hand, it was admirable to give up a comfortable life for one of Torah, but I completely understood the kid. The parents had chosen to live like this, but it wasn't fair to impose such a lifestyle on a boy who had become used to a different way of life.

I felt bad for the parents. They so much wanted a *frum*, wholesome family, but I knew that by demanding any more they would lose Yanky completely.

I suggested that Yanky and his parents make a deal. They wouldn't push him at all, and he would keep wearing his yarmulke and take things at his own pace.

Baruch Hashem, it worked. Yanky slowly took a liking to Judaism, as long as he wasn't being pushed, and today, several years later, he is happily married to a religious girl and brings much *nachas* to his parents.

Such a situation could occur in any *frum* family, even the most well-known and distinguished. However, it seems to happen with more frequency to the children of *ba'alei teshuvah*.

One explanation is that for the parents this is an unfamiliar way of life, and they may not be completely happy themselves. They may know intellectually that they have made the right choice, and they will do all they can to live a *frum* lifestyle, but their children may sense this lack of joy and resent it. Sometimes, as a result, they leave the religious fold.

Additionally, the parents' new acquaintances are different from them, having been born *frum*, and while an adult can deal with these obstacles, a child has more difficulty with it.

The Peter Pan Syndrome

I couldn't help noticing Yankel Ber, a thirty-year-old who lived in my neighborhood. He was often to be found in the *beis midrash*, but hardly ever in his seat. The ultimate fidgeter, he was always shmoozing, walking around, or playing with gadgets. He just couldn't sit down and learn for any length of time.

He once told me that his father had been an old-style European *rav* who had made him learn while other kids played outside. They once went to visit the Steipler Gaon, and the Steipler said to Yankel Ber's father, "I want to tell you something. If you don't let your child play now, he will play later, but play he must!"

His father, he said, decided to ignore the Steipler's advice, and the results were now obvious.

A Slip of the Tongue?

Gabe Nathan came from an observant home, but he had a tough background, including an abusive father and a dysfunctional family. Before he came to the yeshivah, he had really had his ups and downs. He carried a physical scar from when his father had attacked him with a broken bottle and no shortage of emotional scars as well.

One day he mentioned his deceased father to me and added the words *yemach shemo* (may his name be erased).

"What did you say?" I exclaimed.

"I said, '*Yemach shemo*.' What's wrong, Rabbi? Isn't that what you say when your parent is dead?"

"No. You say '*zichrono livrachah*' (may his memory be blessed)."

"Oh, right, that's what I meant. I got mixed up."

Maybe that was what he meant, but I couldn't help thinking of the irony displayed by the Freudian slip. Abuse begets abuse.

Child Razing

My wife was witness to a truly heartrending incident. It happened at a birthday party in my daughter's play group. The custom was that on a child's birthday the girl's mother would bake a cake and bring it to the play group for a little birthday party.

When my daughter's birthday arrived, my wife made cupcakes and bought some other nosh. After the kids ate their regular lunch, the teacher began distributing the food. Everyone made a *berachah* together and started munching when suddenly the teacher jumped up, ran over to one of the little girls, and grabbed her cupcake.

My wife grew alarmed and asked if everything was all right. Was there a health problem? The teacher said, "No, no health problem, but this girl's mother insists that I should not give her daughter any sweets. She is very health-conscious, and she doesn't want her children eating junk."

My wife said, "That's very commendable, but how can you take away her nosh when everyone else is eating? This poor little girl is crying, and everyone else is having fun. What would it hurt if you would let her eat the cupcake, especially since she already received it?"

The teacher replied, "I know. I feel terrible. But I did give her some nosh once, out of pity, and her mother came in and yelled at me for doing it."

There was nothing my wife could do, but she was very upset. How could a mother be so unfeeling, so rigid in her rules, that she would let her child suffer like this? Didn't she realize what this could do to a kid?

The next part of the birthday party was the singing, which took place in the adjoining room. During the singing, the teacher realized that Sarah, the little girl with the strict mother, was missing. She began searching for her, but Sarah was nowhere to be found.

Finally, after several tense minutes, my wife found little Sarah. She was crawling under the table, eating the scraps that had fallen from the other children's cupcakes. She hadn't answered when called, afraid that the "mean" adults would take away the nosh again.

The same can be applied to mitzvos and Torah study. If you force your child to do mitzvos before he is ready, you will turn him off.

When I was a student in yeshivah, there was a boy from France in my class. He'd listen to the *shiur*, occasionally contribute a comment, but he never ever used a Gemara. One day I could no longer contain my curiosity, and after class I asked my rebbe, "Rebbe, why doesn't Moshe ever use a Gemara?"

"When Moshe was a boy in France, five years old, his father insisted that every day he sit down and study Gemara. This was while the other kids were playing outside. He developed such a loathing for it that today he can't even look at a Gemara. The fact that at eighteen years old he can even listen to a Gemara class is a giant step for him."

(Note: Most schools don't start teaching Gemara until fifth grade.)

— E. M.

Parents, Siblings, and Other Juicy Kiruv Targets

Sometimes, in the sincere desire to bring their family into the Orthodox fold, a recent *ba'al teshuvah* will push religion too hard and wind up alienating family and friends. This is a mistake. In America, there is no greater sin than to be self-righteous and judgmental. Even when you're right.

With this in mind, I always remind *ba'alei teshuvah* to be respectful of their families and not to push too hard. Even if they are disturbed by their parents' or siblings' secular lifestyle, they must refrain from commenting, because their criticism will only backfire. Newly minted *ba'alei teshuvah* are well advised to wait for their families' curiosity to be piqued and then, and only then, to explain themselves.

Don't be a play-by-play announcer: "Dad, I am now laving my hands to remove evil spirits." This will just make him think you're crazy.

Rather, you should go home and say nothing about your religious practices. Instead, after dinner, get up and do the dishes.

"Matt, why are you doing the dishes?"

"I figured I'd help out, Mom. You look so tired."

After she is revived from her faint, her reaction will be "I don't know what they did to you at that yeshivah, but go back and get some more."

Here's another one:

"Bernie, why do you stand up when I come in?"

"Well, Dad, my rabbis say I have an obligation to honor and respect you."

As with Mom, make sure Dad is sitting down when he hears this.

And then enjoy the flight back to yeshivah.

They Call It Father's Day, Not Son's Day!

A well-known *kiruv* personality often asks his class the following question, and I've borrowed the technique from him and found it to be effective.

He says to a roomful of *ba'alei teshuvah*, "Imagine today is Father's Day. What would you get your father as a present?"

Invariably some ninety percent will answer, "A book on Judaism." The specific book ranges from scholarly volumes to halachic tomes, sometimes philosophy or chassidic books, but it's always something for the betterment of their dad's soul.

After the poll, the teacher admonishes the boys. "What if your dad is into ancient Chinese history? Would you like it if he bought you a great big book on China for your birthday? *The Influence of Reflective Taoism upon Early Pagodan Architecture*.

"You'd hate it, even if it was released by China's ArtScroll with a convenient English translation. Well, that's about how much he wants to read *How to Legally Separate Cucumbers from Tomatoes on Shabbos and the High Holidays*. It may be fascinating to you, but it isn't fascinating to him."

If members of your family have expressed an interest in aspects of Judaism, then by all means you can discuss theology, lend them books on Judaism, and bring them to Torah classes. But until then, pushing what they see as superstitious, medieval practices will only be counterproductive.

Bottom line: Don't impose your interests on your family.

Shkoiach, Baruch Hashem, and the Blind Hara

I think every passport should have a stamp that says, BEWARE OF YESHIVISH EXPRESSIONS. This way freshly minted *ba'alei teshuvah* will see the stamp on their way home to visit their parents and will be reminded to avoid using yeshivish lingo.

One mother lamented to me, "He used to say thank you. Now he responds in Aramaic."

There is a tendency for *frum* people to overuse expressions such as *"im yirtzeh Hashem," "b'ezras Hashem,"* and the like. This can get annoying even to other *frum* people, but to the family of a *ba'al teshuvah*, it is positively mystifying. One person wanted to know what on earth the "blind hara" was, and did only people with large families do it?

Sometimes *ba'alei teshuvah*, because of their fear of not fitting into the community, adopt the *frum* lingo and take it to extremes.

An example:

"Hi, good morning, how are you?"

"Ah, *bli ayin hara.*"

"Are you going to yeshivah this morning?"

"*Bli neder.*"

"Are you planning to speak in a language other than Hebrew and Aramaic?"

"*Im yirtzeh Hashem.*"

This is a big mistake on the part of the *ba'al teshuvah*. It can really put off his parents. They reluctantly send their son to yeshivah, and then he comes home speaking only Hebrew and Aramaic. It's frightening to them. What happened to their articulate Ivy Leaguer? He sounds like a foreigner.

A rabbi in America related that when his daughter came home from seminary she was constantly saying "*baruch Hashem.*" It was beginning to grate on everyone's nerves.

Finally he told her, "Look, Rav Moshe Feinstein is a big tzaddik. He doesn't say '*baruch Hashem*' in every sentence. You don't have to either. I am not putting down the practice when used appropriately. It is definitely a sign of *eidelkeit* in speech, but please, there's a limit."

Personally I've decided not to use these expressions unless the situation really calls for it, blind neder.

Pesky Little Brother

Ilan Reichman came to Ohr Somayach from a Modern Orthodox home. He had attended a yeshivah high school, and he "frummed out," as they say. Ilan wasn't the first kid in his family to do so. His older brother Stewart had "frummed out" before him.

The first time Ilan went home to visit he stayed for about three weeks. Before he went to yeshivah, he had had a very loving relationship with his parents, but now they seemed distant.

One day Ilan said to his father, "Dad, it seems like you're giving me the cold shoulder. Are you?"

"You're absolutely right. I am."

"Why?"

"Because you make me uncomfortable with your religion."

"Well, what about Stewart? He became religious a long time ago, and you don't give him a cold shoulder."

"The difference is that Stewart may be religious, but he doesn't make me uncomfortable with it."

It seemed that Ilan would correct his father when he washed for meals, would comment on the speed of his father's davening, and similar annoying nitpicks. He didn't realize that the only way he'd be *mekarev* anyone was through his own positive example, not through criticism.

A Better Letter

Sol Weller asked me to review a letter he had written to his parents. After reading just a few lines, I could see the direction in which he was heading.

Having had a secular upbringing and discovering the truth and beauty of Torah later in life, his letter was full of complaints and accusations against his parents for depriving him of his heritage.

This was not the first time I had come across this sort of sentiment, and I applied a technique I had been taught by one of my colleagues. I allowed Sol to articulate his grievances, which were essentially that his parents had raised him without any Torah values. Then I asked him how he had made the change from being secular to becoming *frum*, and he said, "I was searching for truth, and when I found it, I grabbed it and didn't let go."

"Would you say that searching for truth is a Torah value?"

"What kind of question is that, Rabbi? Of course it's a Torah value. What could be more Torah-like than seeking the truth?"

"And who instilled that value in you, to seek truth?"

"Well, I guess it was my parents. They do have a lot of integrity, Rabbi. They are very honest people."

"Really, Sol?"

"Oh yes. Truthfulness was considered very important and was always stressed in my house."

"Well, Sol. I think we should reexamine the facts. Your parents, who themselves were raised without a Torah background, nevertheless instilled in you the one Torah value they possessed, that of seeking the truth, which actually led you to a full Torah life. Perhaps instead of sending this letter, you should write a new one thanking them for helping you discover your heritage."

"I hear you, Rabbi. Let me think about this a little more."

He thought about it and wrote an entirely different letter.

There is another great benefit to writing such a letter. Parents who are thanked by their children for having taught them to seek the truth will certainly not say, "Who me? I didn't emphasize truth and integrity in my house." They will be happy to receive the credit for this positive trait and will thus more readily accept their child's Torah commitment, since it stemmed from their parenting.

A Hole in One

A colleague of mine in Ohr Somayach told me that a young man asked him how he should act when he goes home to visit.

The rabbi said, "Make sure you play golf with your father."

"But, Rabbi, I hate golf."

"But your father likes golf, right? So the best thing you can do is play golf with him."

The kid was home for a couple of weeks and played golf with his father every day, detesting every minute of it. When he was about to board the plane back to Israel, his father said, "You know, Mike, I respect you."

Now that's *kiruv*.

Positive Feedback

POSITIVE FEEDBACK

Everyone likes a compliment. No matter what your profession, at times the daily grind can really get to you. You start to wonder if you're really accomplishing anything, if anyone really gives a hoot. At times like these, a little appreciation can provide a real pick-me-up. A simple compliment or a thank you can carry a person through the day.

This is especially true of any kind of communal work, where the financial rewards are negligible if any, the work is difficult, and the results are not always immediately discernible. Aside from all that, public service often goes unnoticed, as though the chairs in shul somehow arrange themselves in neat rows, and the Shabbos *kiddush* prepares and serves itself after davening. A little well-placed acknowledgment of a person's efforts is often the only payment he can expect to receive, and a sincere compliment goes a long way.

I'm not advising anyone to get involved in community service for the sake of receiving thanks — he's more likely to get compliments of the backhanded variety. Once, a student, on his way out of a well-prepared class, turned to me and said, "Great class, Rabbi. I really needed that nap!"

But on the rare occasions that one's efforts are acknowledged, it feels good.

Oh, THAT Rabbi Kaplan!

Even on the occasions when you feel as though your labors are being acknowledged, it can sometimes backfire.

I spoke one Friday night at a shul in my neighborhood. After the speech, a kid came over to me and asked, "Are you Rabbi Kaplan?"

"Yes."

"Do you teach in Ohr Somayach?"

"Yes."

"Oh, my gosh, I've heard so much about you. I'm so excited to finally meet you."

Trying to control my rapidly swelling head, I said, "Oh, really? Who told you about me?"

"Two of your former *talmidim*, Dov Goodman and Menachem Shenker. They can't stop raving about you."

I searched for the names in my mental telephone directory, trying desperately to hang on to this plaudit, but for the life of me I couldn't remember either name.

"Are you sure they mentioned studying by me?"

By now the boy was somewhat confused. "Aren't you Rav Naftali Kaplan?" — a prominent *mashgiach* and *maggid shiur* in Ohr Somayach.

"Um...no, I'm Dovid Kaplan."

"Oh, in that case, never mind!"

There was an audible hiss as the air left my rapidly deflating head.

It was a long walk home.

The Endgame

I was giving a lecture, and there were about twenty minutes left. The audience seemed interested in the subject, and I felt it was going well.

"Any questions?"

A hand shot up in the back.

"Yes, sir?"

"Uh, Rabbi, what time does class end?"

I guess it wasn't going quite as well as I thought.

Actually, Rick...Thank YOU!

Rick Peterson taught me a lesson about expressing gratitude that I'll never forget. Rick was from South Africa, and, characteristic of South Africans, he was soft-spoken and considerate. But Rick took it to a whole new level.

After the first *shiur* he attended, Rick came up to me and said, "Thank you for the lesson, Rabbi," gave me a warm smile, and left. The next day, again a warm smile and, "Thank you for the lesson, Rabbi." Every single day for as long as he was in my class, I got that smile and a thank you.

One would think I would get tired of the same ritual every day, but I didn't. It felt good every time. Rick made me realize the power of expressing one's appreciation. When someone works at something, he never gets tired of being appreciated and acknowledged.

So, Rick, thank you for the lesson.

Kosher Chuckles

I was heading out of the office one afternoon when a young man with a luxuriant reddish beard and a black hat stopped me.

"Hi, Rabbi Kaplan, *shalom aleichem*."

"Hi, *aleichem shalom*."

I realized he must be a former *talmid* who had grown some facial hair, but I couldn't make out who it was. I tried to imagine the face without the beard, but I just couldn't place him. He smiled at my confusion. Suddenly it hit me.

"Oh no. No way! No way!"

He laughed.

"Meir!"

We hugged and chatted for a few minutes, catching up on the last two years, and then I continued on my way, shaking my head in amazement.

It wasn't the first time Meir had had a good chuckle at my expense. My mind drifted back to two years earlier. Meir had joined a special program in the yeshivah for kids on the fringe. After a very unsuccessful day-school career, Meir had taken to the streets, where he was involved in all sorts of shenanigans and money-making schemes. He made his way to Israel and continued his offbeat career in the Holy Land, eventually joining this program in yeshivah, where it was hoped he'd get his life back on track.

One day I walked into *shiur* and noticed he looked very spaced out. I asked, "What's wrong, Meir? Are you feeling all right?"

"Yeah, sure, Rabbi. I just lost twenty-four thousand dollars on a bad deal, so I'm a little bugged out."

I didn't believe him. After all, what kind of deal could an eighteen-year-old be involved in that would net that sort of cash?

"But it's not so bad. I managed to get eight thousand back."

More talk, I thought. *He needs to be called on it.* "Meir, let's quit telling stories and learn some Torah."

"Rabbi, I'm telling you the truth. You know what? Come up to my dorm room for a second."

We went up to his room, and he retrieved his jacket, which was carelessly draped over a chair. He reached into an inside pocket and removed the thickest wad of hundred-dollar bills I had ever seen. I counted them. Eighty big ones. Meir just stood there and chuckled. I was sweating. I had never seen that much money in one place in my life.

Where and how an eighteen-year-old got that kind of money I never found out — but it certainly wasn't kosher.

Meir went back to the States, turned his life around, and resurfaced as a fully committed Torah Jew. And now he was back, having come full circle, once again having a good chuckle at my expense.

Let him laugh. I'm laughing with him.

All Rise!

One of my classes is a daily *shiur* in *Chumash* for about fifteen to twenty students. Every day, as I enter the room, one guy proclaims in deep bailiff-like tones, "All rise for the rabbi." The first couple of days everyone chuckled, and then the joke started to get a little stale. But human nature is a funny thing, I guess. I missed the announcement the first day the bailiff was absent and not everyone stood up.

From Ignoramus to Ignorer

"Hey, look, Mom, there's a rabbi of mine from Ohr Somayach! Rabbi, I'm getting married next month. Why don't you come to the wedding?"

This was from a former student of mine named Jeffrey, whom I hadn't seen in about a year. He noticed me walking down the main street in Meah Shearim and decided to invite me to his weddings. How quaint. Any teacher will tell you that the lifeblood of his profession is the achievement of his students, and his professional adrenaline is the appreciation students show for the teacher's effort and accomplishment.

This is particularly true with the type of teaching found in a yeshivah, where a rebbe is not only an imparter of knowledge, but a mentor, confidant, advisor, and provider of a good meal on Shabbos.

This relationship tends to create an emotional closeness and a bond well beyond that of a college professor and his students. Usually a student with whom one has connected will stay in touch by calling before holidays and during family celebrations. While not an official part of the job description, it is one of the fringe benefits that makes teaching Torah so rewarding.

The flip side of the coin is that when a student with whom one feels particularly close seems to ignore your contributions or to forget about you, it hurts that much more.

Jeffrey in particular was a guy I had really put a lot of work into, both in his studies and in his private life. I had watched him go from an ambition-free loafer to a serious, goal-oriented mensch.

After he graduated my class, he stayed on in yeshivah for some time, and then one day he just disappeared, no goodbye, nothing. I never heard from Jeffrey again, until about a year later, when I heard a rumor that he was engaged to be married. I figured he would certainly contact me shortly to catch me up on his life. But I didn't hear from him, nor did I receive a wedding invitation. And then the above-mentioned encounter. I was invited as an afterthought.

I went home very upset. I did not attend his wedding.

There was a similar incident with another fellow, but he sent me an actual invitation, not for the main ceremony and meal, mind you, but for the dancing afterward.

That's the invitation you usually reserve for your roommate's second cousin, not for someone who has had a major influence on your life.

Again I didn't attend the wedding.

I would like to think the reason was to teach these boys sensitivity and to have a little more appreciation for those who helped them.

I'd like to think that. But that's not it. I was just hurt.

Hal Davis is another story completely. When Hal entered the yeshivah, he and I hit it off immediately, and we became very close. Eventually he became *frum*, married a nice girl, and left the yeshivah to earn a living. Despite his very busy life, he didn't sever his ties to his teachers, and he stays in touch, calls me every *erev yom tov* and whenever he has a family *simchah*. Hal is the kind of *talmid* who makes being in this business very gratifying.

Shidduchim

SHIDDUCHIM

One of the areas of religious life in which *ba'alei teshuvah* require a great deal of assistance is in finding a spouse the Orthodox way, through what we call *shidduchim*. Finding a *shidduch*, for several reasons, presents a recent *ba'al teshuvah* with some of the toughest challenges he will encounter in his newfound observant lifestyle.

A little primer for the uninitiated: In Orthodox Jewish life, boys and girls are strongly discouraged from meeting and mingling socially once they have reached the stage of puberty. Obviously this restriction might create a bit of difficulty in finding one's life's companion when that time arrives. And singles' bars, despite the high-quality relationships that might arise there, are not the solution, so what to do?

The answer, developed and refined over many centuries of traditional and harmonious living, is *shidduchim*. An outside party introduces a young couple to each other in a dignified manner, and they set about discovering if they are compatible. If they like each other, and their ideals and life goals match, they may decide to get engaged and married. There is little of the hit-and-miss dating found in today's society; dating is a serious endeavor, with the goal being, not just a fun time, but marriage.

There are many different customs and traditions involved in this system, depending on the stream of Orthodoxy one identifies with, but the general idea is the same. The one thing you can be sure of, though, is that the stereotypical matchmaker as town yenta is almost a complete fable. The real system is much more sensitive and complex than has been portrayed by the popular culture.

At Ohr Somayach I found that dating and *shidduchim* are very much a part of the student-faculty interaction. We are usually dealing with boys of marriageable age, and they are usually single when they arrive at yeshivah. Often, after having spent time studying Torah and growing in a spiritual sense, these young men decide that they want to find a partner in life, and they begin getting involved in *shidduchim*.

One common difficulty is that *ba'alei teshuvah* often have little family support and social contacts in the Orthodox community, which makes it more difficult to set them up with appropriate mates. For an FFB boy or girl, most matches are usually introduced by way of family and friends, which for a recent *ba'al teshuvah* may not be a very large circle.

In addition, a *ba'al teshuvah* is accustomed to secular dating, and he needs to reconsider his whole approach for the *shidduch* scene. As one young man once said to me, "Rabbi, I want to go out on a *shidduch* just to see what it's like." The young man was not committed to marriage or even to *Yiddishkeit*, and I had to explain to him, "Listen, Jeff, *shidduchim* is not 'dating to see what it's like.' We are playing for keeps here. If you go out, you may end up getting married to this person, and, quite frankly, you're not interested in that right now."

Another difficulty *ba'alei teshuvah* face is a result of their very diversity. While this makes for interesting personalities, varied backgrounds are often a disadvantage in *shidduchim*. Take, for example, a religious young man from Bnei Brak and a young woman from Geulah. Their backgrounds and lifestyles are so similar that after two or three meetings they can be reasonably confident that they have found their intended. *Ba'alei teshuvah*, on the other hand, have such varied backgrounds that they need much more time to get to know one another and can encounter many more obstacles to compatibility.

To counter the lack of connections and the various other difficulties, the staff at Ohr Somayach and other *ba'al teshuvah* yeshivos provide the young men with a great deal of assistance in this area and are extremely dedicated toward helping each young man find his destined mate. Most yeshivos even retain specific staff members whose job descriptions include the title *shidduchim* advisor.

They are available for counsel, as a shoulder to cry on, and, most importantly, to do the actual legwork that goes into every *shidduch* — making phone calls, checking out suggestions, and, often, providing a place for the young couple to meet for the first time.

The question that always arises, both in class and from shocked parents, is this: "How can you possibly marry someone you've known for such a short period of time?" They would usually prefer that the young couple live together for a while before getting serious.

In truth, according to the statistics, there is a far greater divorce rate among couples who have lived together before getting married than among those who have not. This can be explained logically any number of ways.

But we don't need the logical explanations; the proof of the pudding is to be seen within the Orthodox community. If you've been around Orthodox Jews, and you've been to their Shabbos tables, you've seen that usually their homes are not full of strife and bickering. Rather, there is warmth, love, and closeness. There is interaction with the children and respect between the parents. They all got married through the *shidduch* system; its success is evident and undeniable.

Give AND Take

I always tell the guys that getting married is taking. People think it's giving. But it's not. It's taking — taking all of one's preconceived notions from Hollywood and the media and flushing them down the drain. This is the type of taking that's required to have a successful marriage.

Like the great Rav Mendel Kaplan often said, "In order to get married, a person has to give up a little selfishness!" A pithy line, but one containing great wisdom.

"But how do I know if I'm ready to get married?" is a common question. Well, as they say, when you want to go out and find your other half, the first thing you've got to do is find your first half. You can't expect to find someone to complement you if you don't even know yourself. If you don't know in which direction you are heading, you can't really expect someone else to accompany you on the journey.

I met a young man on the soccer field, Mike Joseph, so refined, soft-spoken, and respectful. In a classic show of selflessness, despite my sub-par soccer skills, Mike always gave up his opportunity to score and passed me the ball, because, after all, I'm the rabbi. This was not a common thing among the other boys, despite my venerable age, or perhaps due to it.

Mike, with his gentle nature, was well liked in the yeshivah, but for some reason he was having difficulty finding a wife. He went out seven or eight times with one particular girl, but that didn't work out. Another girl he was dating he thought he liked, but it turned out she was seeing someone else simultaneously. It was one tough break after another. Finally Mike met his intended, and they got engaged.

By this time Mike had advanced to a mainstream yeshivah, and we were no longer in close contact. Still, as his rebbe and friend, I received an invitation to the wedding in Bnei Brak.

So about two months later I boarded a bus for Bnei Brak and found my way to the wedding hall, a large one containing two separate ballrooms. I saw a wedding in process and I walked in, but it wasn't Mike's. I found my way to the second hall, but it was empty. No wedding there that night.

As I stood there scratching my head, Mike himself walked into the hall, dressed in casual, weekday clothing. After a somewhat awkward hello, he explained that the engagement had been broken and the wedding called off. Mike just happened to be at the hall that evening, not to get married, but to get his deposit back.

I was heartbroken and rather stunned. I didn't know what to say. But Mike saved me the worry. He looked at me and whispered, "Don't worry, Rabbi. I'm seeing a wonderful girl now, and we hope to be getting engaged soon."

Thankfully this one was the real thing, and Mike was soon engaged and married, and today he is happily settled.

Arranging Shidduchim

It may sound like fun to be the instrument of a successful *shidduch*, and indeed there is a great feeling of accomplishment when one's hard work pays off and a happy couple finds one another due to one's efforts. But one must be careful not to approach this lightly, always in anticipation of a happy, fairy-tale ending. Anyone who gets involved in making *shidduchim*, particularly for *ba'alei teshuvah*, is taking on a tremendous responsibility. One is taking the place that is traditionally assumed by parents and family and must be cognizant of the great responsibility this entails.

Most *ba'alei teshuvah* are in the unenviable position of having no one to help them investigate a prospective spouse and are unusually dependent on outsiders and professional *shadchanim*. Good intentions are important, but an overriding sense of accountability is even more vital.

A young man with whom I am very close came to me and told me he is starting to see a certain young lady. "Rebbe, she's wonderful, and we hit it off very well."

"Has anyone checked out her background?"

"Yes, she's from a good family in Westchester, well established, nothing to worry about."

"How did you meet?"

"Well, she noticed me in the *beis midrash* on Shabbos while I was davening, and she was very impressed."

It sounded like a wonderful story, so I went home and told it to my wife. She was a bit skeptical because she thought the boy's davening wasn't all that special. A warning flag went up, but I figured there was nothing too peculiar about that, so I left it alone.

Then my wife asked me about the girl. I said she came from a fine family, originally from New York. My wife said, "You'd better check into it some more."

"No problem."

I checked into her background, called some teachers, and kept hearing nice things about the girl. Then I spoke to a friend of hers, who told me, "She's terrific. She would do anything for anyone at any time."

Another warning flag went up. Such behavior is extreme and often a compensation for some flaw, such as a lack of self-esteem. I mentioned my misgivings to the boy, but he didn't take them too seriously, so I didn't either, and the *shidduch* proceeded. Each time I spoke to him, he was very positive about her. They had similar goals, that he learn after marriage and they live in Israel.

One Friday I called him, and he told me that they would be seeing each other on Shabbos. I told him that he should call me on *motza'ei Shabbos* to let me know they were engaged. There was no more progress to be made, so why not finish it?

The young man was very excited. He could hardly wait for Shabbos to be over.

Motza'ei Shabbos he called me up. I said, "Hi! Good news?"

He said, "No, not really. We broke it off completely."

"What?! What happened?"

"Well, it turns out that she has a serious medical condition and suffers from extremely low self-esteem. She has a whole slew of problems, psychological and otherwise. She only told me about it tonight."

I was shocked. Why had no one mentioned this to me? The people who knew her didn't say anything about it. They had investigated the boy very closely, but hadn't volunteered any real information about the girl.

I suppose they felt their responsibility was primarily to the girl, not the boy. The problem was, my responsibility was to the boy, and I hadn't done enough.

I learned a hard lesson from this. Nothing can be taken for granted when checking out a *shidduch*. One must look into a student's *shidduch* as if for one's own child.

A Spirited Date

One young man in my *shiur* was having a particularly difficult time with *shidduchim*. Gershon was a good catch, and he was getting dates with one great girl after the other, but usually, after one or two meetings, the girl would break it off. They felt he was too uptight, too nervous. Of course, the more things didn't work out, the more nervous Gershon became.

Finally, after yet another no-go date, he asked me, "Rabbi, why do I keep getting dropped? What am I doing wrong?"

I said, "Look, Gershon, I think you're a little too tense when you go out. You've got to loosen up a little. The feedback from the girls is that you're a nice guy, but a little too uptight. I think it might be a good idea for you to have a drink before the next date. That'll help you loosen up and show your true personality."

"Great idea, Rabbi. That's what I'm gonna do."

A few days later he went out on a date, with a little boost from Johnnie Walker, and the following day I gave him a call.

"*Nu*, Gershon, how did it go?"

"Well, Rabbi, I thought it went well, but she doesn't want to go out anymore. I don't know what went wrong."

I called the *shadchan*, and she told me that the date was great, but the girl was very concerned about something. It seemed she had smelled alcohol on Gershon's breath.

Ooops!

Today Gershon is happily married and, of course, a teetotaler.

Sooner or Later

Avraham had been on the dating scene for quite a while and couldn't seem to find the right girl. He came from a very fine family and was an accomplished scholar, but he was having *shidduch* troubles. One day he came to see me, very upset after going out for so many futile years.

"Rabbi, what am I doing wrong?"

I looked at him in silence. What could I say?

"Rabbi, this is very difficult. I just want to get married. Why don't I get suggested the right kind of *shidduchim*?"

"Yes, it is difficult, Avraham. I know it's frustrating. Sometimes people just don't understand what you're looking for."

What I do say to encourage the young men suffering through *shidduchim* is, "Just remember, there's something uniquely different between this form of misery and any other form of misery. When you're suffering from *shidduchim*, you are always just one telephone call away from meeting your intended. Just one *shadchan* needs to call about someone she would like you to meet. That girl may be the one, and within a few weeks you could be engaged. And then all the troubles that came before are forgotten as though they never existed."

The Talmud says in reference to one's intended, "He who has found a wife has found goodness!" The commentators point out that the Sages use the word *found* to imply that just as one who finds an object does so by chance, by stumbling across it, so it is with *shidduchim* — if you look too hard, you will get frustrated. A degree of laissez faire goes a long way toward relieving the frustration.

A classic story is that of Freddy Goldstein. Originally from Oregon, the Sooner State, Freddy came to Israel and spent a few months studying at Ohr Somayach, where he became committed to a Torah lifestyle. Having left a thriving business behind, however, Freddy was compelled to return to Oregon. While Oregon is assuredly a great place to live, it can get rather lonely for a young man attempting to find an Orthodox Jewish wife. In fact, the only *frum* girl in town happened to be Freddy's sister.

The business was too good to leave, but the loneliness was making it hard to stay. Finally Freddy decided he would take some time off from work and go to Israel to look for a *shidduch*. He made arrangements by phone to meet some promising girls while in Israel, prayed a lot, and arrived in the Holy Land with high hopes.

A week into his trip Freddy said to me, "Rabbi, things aren't going well. I've already met two girls, and there was nobody home!"

I could see he was beginning to get depressed and to give up hope. It may sound like he was giving up too quickly, but he had really pinned his hopes on this trip. All I could say was "Listen, Freddy, just remember that any time the phone rings, it can be your *bashert*."

He nodded halfheartedly, thanked me, and said he would be in touch. Indeed, he was in touch. Later the same day he called. He had gotten a call from a *shadchan*, and the prospective young lady sounded wonderful. They hit it off immediately, and within ten days they were engaged.

I was introduced to the young lady and was amazed at what a good pair the young couple made; they even looked alike. Today they are happily married and living in Oregon.

So while I don't make light of the difficulties confronted in *shidduchim*, it is worthwhile remembering that the right one may be only one phone call away.

Another young man, today happily married, told me he was on the phone with his friend, lamenting his inability to find a *shidduch*. To really brighten up his day, the phone line disconnected right in the middle of his *kvetching*. As he was waiting for his friend to call him back, another person called and suggested that he meet a certain girl. This proposed *shidduch*, amazingly enough, ended up becoming his wife. Like I said, one never knows when that call will come, and from whom.

By the way, if the disconnected guy is out there, your friend is still waiting for you to call back.

Amen — Not Omen!

Another thing that should be emphasized is that *shidduch* dating must be a natural process, meaning that there must be an attraction to each other and a certain amount of common ground. One cannot simply go in blind and trust in fate. A question I hear very often is

"What are the omens or signs that will tell me that a *shidduch* is *bashert*?"

There may be such definite signs, but I certainly don't know what they are, and I always discourage thinking and acting based on so-called omens in the strongest terms.

I've been told a story, which I can't personally vouch for, but I fear it's probably true. A certain young man made the trip to Amukah, the grave of Yonasan ben Uziel. Tradition has it that anyone who goes there and prays for a *shidduch* will be granted assistance. The *neshamah* of Yonasan ben Uziel will daven for him. Or something like that.

On the way to Amukah this young man stopped in Tzefas. He saw a young lady there and was smitten, but, being a religious young man, he couldn't approach her and start talking, so he did nothing and continued on his way.

When he arrived at Amukah, what do you know, just as he got there the very same young lady was just getting out of a taxi, also apparently coming to pray for a *shidduch*.

Our hero spent some time there praying, and when he was done, he saw that someone had left his siddur behind. He checked the inside flap and found a name with a Jerusalem address located not far from his apartment. Wanting to do a good deed, the fellow took the siddur back to Jerusalem with him and went to the address to drop it off. Sure enough, it was the home of this same young lady. A tale worthy of O. Henry or Twain.

He gave her the siddur and left. When he arrived home, he received a phone call from a friend who had a suggestion for a *shidduch*. The girl? None other than his new friend from Amukah.

Two days later another friend called, and he suggested the same *shidduch*.

It was a sign! Obviously they were meant for each other!

Not wanting to fight fate, the boy and girl decided to meet. Two weeks later they were engaged, and two months later they were married.

Six weeks after that they were divorced.

I like telling this story to demonstrate that every step must be carefully thought out and approached with maturity. Of course, it helps to daven at Amukah, and Hashem may bestow upon us amazing signs and coincidences, but to take one's life partner based on omens? Absolutely not.

Ready or Not!

"Hi, Rabbi, can I speak to you for a few moments?"

"Sure, Leonard."

Leonard Alan, a fine young man from South Africa with a background in physical education, had been studying in the yeshivah for a couple of months. As indicated by his career choice, Leonard had a certain energetic streak. Full-time learning was probably not on the horizon for him. He needed to be doing something active. Leonard had already attained his college degree and started a successful business, and now he wanted to know what he should do next. Should he continue learning and stay in the yeshivah or go back and get his master's?

After we discussed his situation at length, I realized that what Leonard really wanted to do was to get married. He just didn't know it yet.

So I brought it up.

"Leonard, do you think you're ready for marriage?"

"Oh no, Rabbi, definitely not. I don't think I can get married yet. I'm too selfish."

"Leonard, that may be the best sign that you are ready for marriage. If you recognize that you're selfish, and you are ready to work on it, you can get married. The one thing marriage helps to cure is selfishness. It's not automatic, but nothing provides a framework for working on selfishness like marriage. Certainly remaining a bachelor will not help you become less selfish. To the contrary, the people who feel completely ready usually aren't."

Age is not the only factor in determining if one is ready for marriage.

An even more important factor is whether or not a person is responsible and willing to grow. Marriage demands a large degree of responsibility and provides a marvelous environment for growth. But one has to know what he's getting into. If a person is irresponsible, he or she should not get married. It's that simple.

But if one is selfish or self-centered, that's exactly what marriage does cure.

Blame It on the In-Laws

This is a story I couldn't make up if I wanted to. A group of kids was visiting the yeshivah for the summer, and whenever we have a group of nonreligious Jews visiting, we always try to bring them to an Orthodox wedding or a bris so they can experience a *frum* celebration firsthand.

As luck would have it, one of the boys in the yeshivah was getting married that night, and we wangled dinner invitations for all our guests. On the day of the wedding I gave a talk to the boys on how a religious wedding is conducted and presented a general overview of dating and marriage in traditional Judaism. Among other things, we discussed what they would see at the wedding — the bride walking around the groom seven times, the groom breaking the glass in mourning, and the lively dancing, the men and women separately. I contrasted this with the secular idea of a wedding — mixed dancing, too much alcohol, and a more raucous atmosphere. I told them that at this wedding they would see everyone in control while still having a good time. One would never see rowdiness or drunkenness at a *frum* wedding. This reflected the Jewish idea that a wedding is a joyous and holy occasion.

One young man at Ohr Somayach had previously worked as the lighting technician for a well-known photographer in New York. This boy's job was to hold and position the lights for the photographer. One night they had a job at an Italian wedding. As they walked in through the back door, they noticed a pool of blood at the threshold. They figured it must be animal blood and were wondering if this was some Old Country marriage custom when the police arrived.

The explanation turned out to be rather simple. This was the spot where the groom's friends had beaten up the caterer for not providing enough whiskey.

The same fellow worked one night at an Irish wedding, and as the party drew to a close he noticed the bride sitting alone at the head table crying her eyes out. What happened was that the groom had gotten stone drunk and ended up locked in the bathroom for four hours, and no one knew where he was. This is definitely not something you would see at a Torah wedding.

I also told the boys that the bride and groom fast on their wedding day and seek forgiveness for their sins in order to enter this new phase of their lives as pure, cleansed new people. The Jewish wedding day is a private Yom Kippur for the bride and groom, not just a tension-filled time before a wild party.

I also contrasted the ideas of who is entertaining whom at the wedding. At a *frum* wedding, everyone is there to cheer the bride and groom and to make this day the most special one of their lives, whereas a secular wedding is more of a social occasion, with the bride and groom going from table to table greeting everyone and making sure the guests are sufficiently entertained.

That night we all went to the wedding together, ate something at the smorgasbord, and then went outside to see the *chuppah*. (In Israel, the *chuppah* is often held outside, under the stars.) The guys got very excited every time they recognized one of the customs we had discussed, and everyone was having a great time.

After the *chuppah* we went inside for the dinner, where our group was seated at one large table. We were just remarking on how beautiful it was when we heard the sound of crashing glass and people shouting. Suddenly the *mechitzah* tumbled over, and we saw a wild melee in the women's section. Fists were flying and ladies were screaming. Eventually someone was dragged out of the room and calm was restored.

It turned out that a drunk had come in off the street and decided to join the party. He went straight to the ladies' side to make trouble, and they had to wrestle him out of there.

The guys wanted to know if this was also a beautiful and holy Jewish custom.

Ouch! You're Shuckeling Too Hard!

OUCH! YOU'RE SHUCKELING TOO HARD!

One of the hardest things for a *ba'al teshuvah* to master is the ability to be religious and become closer to God, yet at the same time to remain a mensch in his relationships with others. I've observed that occasionally a person who has spent his life involved in material pursuits and has suddenly become interested in spiritual values may go slightly overboard in his commitment. He can become so involved in proper religious observance that he might unwittingly trample on the next person on the way to performing his mitzvah. This behavior, in addition to creating a social misfit, is also a *chillul Hashem*, a desecration of God's Name, and renders the good deed worthless.

An extreme example is the guy who swings his tzitzis so hard that he whips the next guy in the eye. To employ a more common, and more annoying, example, there's the guy who practices his shofar-blowing at two in the morning so he can be ready for Rosh HaShanah services. We all get turned off at such behavior, so what I always tell my students is "Don't be too *frum*. Remember to be considerate."

Rabbi Yisrael Salanter once said that a person could destroy an entire world while running to do a mitzvah. So to all *ba'alei teshuvah*, and FFB's as well, I advise, walk fast, don't run.

Being Holy...Not!

One Friday night I was eating over at a friend's house. The host was an FFB and a somewhat learned man who had studied in advanced yeshivos for quite a few years.

I was not the only guest. In addition to myself, they had invited a newly married couple, both *ba'alei teshuvah*.

The host greeted the guests, sang *Shalom Aleichem*, and made Kiddush. As we sat down to eat, the host inquired of the young groom, "So tell me, Yaakov, what is it that you do?" An innocent question, I thought.

"I'm sorry, I don't discuss my work on Shabbos."

This assertion was followed by a rather uncomfortable silence, with no one being quite sure what to say next. It was really not a very classy move on the part of the guest, to say the least.

This was a classic example of a newly religious young man who did not understand that despite the prohibitions against discussing specific aspects of one's work on Shabbos, it is entirely permissible to divulge one's occupation, and then, if pressed for details, to gently, tactfully, change the subject. Even if one wishes to completely avoid workaday topics on the holy Shabbos, one must understand that it is far worse to make someone feel foolish than to say, "Oh, I'm a carpenter."

Social graces are not discarded simply because one becomes more devoted to God.

Praying on Other People

Aside from my work with bona fide *ba'alei teshuvah*, I did some time as a *mashgiach* in a mainstream American yeshivah for several years. This particular yeshivah was geared to post-high-school American boys who came to study in Israel for further spiritual development.

Many of the students came from Modern Orthodox homes. After studying in the yeshivah for a while, they returned to America with a somewhat more yeshivish outlook on life than when they had left.

Very often, before vacation, guys would ask me if, when they go back home, they should lead the prayers in shul and "slow down the davening." Their families davened in Modern Orthodox shuls where they usually polish off *shacharis* in half an hour. If the guys led the davening, they could slow it down to forty-five minutes. They wanted to know if they would be doing a mitzvah by giving the congregation more time to concentrate on the prayers.

I always told the boys that the only thing they would succeed in doing was to antagonize the rest of the congregation. They had no right to push their newfound piety on anyone else. If they really wanted to do some good, they should let someone else lead the prayers and focus on improving their own concentration in prayer. But to take their own religious commitment, which was indeed a wonderful thing, and rub someone else's nose in it, would not only be ineffective; it would negate the spiritual component for themselves as well. As Rabbi Yisrael Salanter once said, "Concern for your friends' *gashmiyus* is your own *ruchniyus*."

Too Much of a Good Thing

Zev Terren, formerly known as William, was a really fine, well-mannered young man. He was also good-looking and had a pleasant nature, but, strangely enough, he was not successful when it came to *shidduchim*. In most respects Zev was a private kind of fellow, even somewhat reserved, but for some reason he would readily discuss all aspects of his dating life with roommates, friends, and strangers he met on the bus.

The rebbes in yeshivah advised him not to talk about it so much, but it didn't help. He would open up to anyone who would listen.

One day Zev came to see me and really poured out his heart about his dating ordeals. He described all the *shidduchim* that looked right but didn't pan out and the ones that were suggested but were completely wrong. There were more than a few girls Zev had been sure were the right ones, and then either he or the girl had a sudden change of heart. I listened sympathetically for over an hour, trying to help him work through his frustration and offering advice where appropriate.

Before he left the office, I said to him, "Listen, Zev, I do have one suggestion to make to you. It may not solve the problem, but it's something to consider in any case. Maybe you shouldn't discuss your dating so much. The Talmud advises that success is usually found in that which is hidden. Not every acquaintance of yours has to know every detail of your *shidduchim*."

Perhaps a week later I bumped into Zev in the hallway, and I said, "So, Zev, anything happening in *shidduchim?*"

He looked me squarely in the eye and said, "Yes, as a matter of fact, there is, but I can't tell you about it, Rabbi. I've decided not to discuss it."

I smiled at what I thought was a cute quip, but it wasn't a quip at all. He was perfectly serious. I could not believe my ears.

While I was elated that finally someone was following my advice, I began to get an inkling of why this fellow couldn't quite tie the knot.

That Is Disgusting!

When I was a student in the yeshivah, I was sitting in the dining room at lunch one day and had just washed *mayim acharonim* in preparation for *bentching*. The guy sitting across from me looked over at me and said, "Ugh, that's disgusting."

I said, "What is? What's disgusting?"

"What you just did."

"What'd I do?"

"You washed *mayim acharonim* and dripped some water on the bread over there. That's really disgusting."

I said to him, "You know, you're lucky I'm already *frum*, because if I wasn't, people like you would ensure that I'd never become *frum*. I mean, here I am, a newcomer to the faith, and while trying to do a mitzvah, I get insulted by an old-timer."

It's true. I probably would have been so turned off by this guy's rudeness that I would have blamed all Orthodox Jews because of him.

How many times do such things happen, small things we may not even notice, but that an onlooker does notice and as a consequence carries away a poor impression of all religious Jews. We are always on display to the world, and we are judged by a very exacting standard.

Not for nothing do our Sages tell us that a Torah scholar's behavior must be beyond reproach. There are behaviors that may be acceptable for the rest of the world but, when a Torah scholar is involved, constitute a sacrilege.

A Sorry Situation

There are certain Yiddish words that have been picked up by the general English-speaking public, words like *chutzpah*, *mensch*, and *nudnik*. Everyone knows it's important to be a mensch and not to have too much chutzpah. I'd like to add another caution: don't be a nudnik.

I was in attendance at a crowded, beautiful wedding, intently focused on the acrobatics being performed in front of the *chasan* and *kallah*, when I felt a tap on the shoulder. I turned around, and this fellow said to me, "I'm sorry." I didn't know him, but I could tell from his attire that he was a recent *ba'al teshuvah*.

"What are you sorry for?"

"I bumped into you."

"Oh, okay. No problem."

A few minutes later, another tap on the shoulder.

"Yeah?"

"I apologize."

"For what?"

"I accidentally knocked you with my elbow."

Two minutes later, yet another tap on the shoulder. "Sorry for banging into you."

I wanted to tell the guy, "Look, you are obviously working on becoming a more sensitive person, and that's an admirable goal, but in the meantime, you're succeeding in being an absolute pain in the neck." I said nothing, but moved elsewhere so that others could also be lucky recipients of his sensitivity.

The not uncommon "I'm-working-on-myself-and-I-want-others-to-notice" syndrome is one I have found advisable to suppress. It annoys people and it doesn't work. As our Sages say, "He who runs from honor will ultimately receive honor. One who pursues it will have it flee from him."

The surest way to impress is by not trying to impress. The surest way to get noticed is by trying not to be noticed. And if you try not to be noticed as a way of getting noticed, that will be noticed, too. There's more to say on this subject, but for the sake of retaining our sanity, we'll stop right here.

Strange Practices

I've found that it is also a good idea to avoid doing anything strange in one's service of Hashem, even involving only oneself. The Torah has been around a couple thousand years, and there are certain things that are accepted in the mainstream and certain things that aren't.

This is a good concept for any area of life, but particularly in Torah Judaism, where every detail of observance has been keenly scrutinized under the halachic microscope. It's foolish to assume you've discovered something everyone else has overlooked. It's fine to discover the realm of halachah for oneself and to question the whys and wherefores, but I always tell the guys, "Before you begin a new practice, check with your teacher or mentor to see if it's worthwhile."

I walked into the *beis midrash* one day for *minchah*, and there were two young men davening *minchah* in *talleisim*. Apparently they had wanted to pray wearing jackets, as per convention, but they couldn't find their jackets, so they decided to don *talleisim*. Technically there is nothing wrong with this, but the accepted custom has always been to wear *talleisim* only during morning prayers. The resident halachic authority approached them and said that if they would like to cover their arms during davening, then they must go upstairs and find their jackets, but they may not daven *minchah* wearing *talleisim*.

"Why not, Rabbi? It's not forbidden, is it?"

"No, but it's strange, and we don't look to do strange things. Besides, in a yeshivah people can be easily influenced, and the next thing you know, we'll have half the yeshivah davening *minchah* in their *talleisim*."

A Rosy Arrangement

Greg Forsham was doing great in yeshivah. He was really starting to learn, was enjoying his newfound *Yiddishkeit*, and was a pleasure to have in *shiur*. One day he approached me after *shacharis* and said, "Rabbi, my mom's finally making peace with my being in yeshivah. In fact, she's coming to visit me today."

"Oh, that's great. So you're going to meet her at the airport?"

"Actually, no. She'll take a taxi. I don't want to miss *shiur*."

Hmm, I thought. *It looks like this peace treaty with his learning is about to be broken.*

"Listen, Greg, not only are you not allowed in *shiur* today, but you're going to the florist right now to buy your mom a bunch of flowers and meet her at the airport. Now get moving."

Again, sometimes you have to sacrifice your own spiritual advancement for the sake of *menschlichkeit*. After all, one of the primary goals of spiritual attainment is just that — to become a true mensch. So it's not a sacrifice, but an application of what you're learning in yeshivah.

Besides, in the long run it will usually pay off even in additional spiritual gains, when one's family realizes that this religion thing makes one, not a fanatic, but a better person in all respects.

Unexpected Reactions

UNEXPECTED REACTIONS

As a religious rabbi in a secular world, I try to be ready for all sorts of situations, but every now and then the things I say and do can provoke some really unexpected reactions.

This happened during a visit to America at a shul that was, at least on paper, Orthodox. The actual level of the members' religious observance ranged from marginally observant to completely noncommitted, and there I was, an ultra-Orthodox extremist from Jerusalem, speaking to this group on Shabbos about the Torah.

More than anything I wanted to shatter the stereotype of the so-called black hat community as being insular, unenlightened fanatics. Obviously, a fire-and-brimstone sermon was not the way to go with this audience. After giving it a lot of thought, I decided that the best way to approach the situation would be to show off my secular knowledge, how hip we Orthodox Jews are, while at the same time communicating some Torah message.

This happened to take place during the Olympic competitions, and all one could read about in the newspaper and hear on the news was the Olympics and the athletes competing in them. So I decided to speak about the Oneness of Hashem and His uniqueness, and I used the Olympics as a metaphor — the idea of striving to be number one, the most unique.

I felt it was a good speech. I got some good jokes about the Olympics in there and a serious message as well, and all in all I was pretty pleased with my performance. The audience also seemed to have enjoyed the talk. At least, no one actually pulled out a pillow.

After davening ended, I was approached by a little old man with a thick Yiddish accent.

"Y'know, boychik, dat vas ah excellent spitch. I can see you really vatched a lot of de Alympics on TV."

So much for shattering stereotypes.

Daffy Definition

One young lady came to my house as a guest for Shabbos lunch. This girl was nonobservant, but her sister had become a *ba'alas teshuvah* and was now trying to convince her sibling to look into Judaism.

The young lady had read a book called *A Tzaddik in Our Time*, the story of Rav Aryeh Levine, one of the most remarkable people of this century, a man known for his absolute humility and selfless kindness to all, irrespective of race or religion. It is quite impossible to read that book and not come away feeling awed that such a tzaddik existed.

Or so I thought.

This girl, due to her knee-jerk disapproval of her sister's *Yiddishkeit*, saw it differently. "You know what? I think that Rabbi Levine is one of the most selfish people I've ever come across."

"Really. How so?" I wasn't feeling quite as polite inside.

"Well, don't you believe that for every act of kindness you get eternal reward?"

"Yes."

"So don't you think that's selfish? Spending one's entire life trying to grab as much reward as possible."

I suppose I could have explained to her that the very purpose of God's creating this world was so that people should receive reward, thus making the pursuit of Heavenly reward the very fulfillment of God's will. Hardly an act of selfishness.

Additionally, we have no idea what Rabbi Levin's motivations were, and he probably was not thinking of any reward when he went to visit thieves and hoodlums in the dank British dungeons. A scholar of great renown, he could have "grabbed" just as much "selfish" reward in the *beis midrash*, in the company of his learned compatriots.

These explanations are the truth.

But the truth, of course, was beside the point. The real problem was this incredibly bizarre definition of *selfish*. This girl would never have described Mother Theresa, the gentile world's exemplar of kindliness, as selfish or reward-seeking.

Only Rabbi Aryeh Levin, an Orthodox Jew, is subjected to this kind of convoluted reasoning, where good is bad and bad is wonderful.

In truth, the possibilities are endless. Ebenezer Scrooge, the standard for cruel, greedy behavior, now becomes the paragon of altruism by virtue of never having helped anyone. John D. Rockefeller was a great guy for most of his life, until he messed up at the end and started giving charity.

Ludicrous beyond words.

Tape Delay

For anyone wishing to go into *kiruv*, or any form of public speaking, I would like to mention a potential pitfall that I have encountered. In fact, I fell right into the pit.

While tapes can be a marvelous teaching tool and can help one reach a much larger audience than live classes, there are certain dangers that one must be aware of when recording a lecture. This was brought home to me when I received an anonymous letter berating me for my callous disregard for other people's feelings.

"Don't you know that Chazal say? 'He who shames his fellow in public has no share in the World to Come.' How could you be so indifferent to another person's feelings?" The letter writer mentioned a specific tape of mine, but did not specify what I had said that so upset him.

I remembered the *shiur* in question. It was on the subject of eating non-kosher food, but I could not recall insulting anyone, so I immediately headed to the tape library to find the offensive statement.

After listening to most of the recording, I finally found the only thing the writer could have been referring to. During a discussion about applying holiness to commonplace things, such as our eating habits, I commented on the need to maintain self-control even with respect to kosher food, such as not eating in a gluttonous manner. Several students chuckled at this, and two boys, who were especially close *talmidim* of mine, actually laughed aloud.

I gave them a look of mock severity and said, "Boy, if I've ever seen guilt written on someone's face!"

It was clearly meant as a joke, and everyone there took it as such and laughed uproariously. No one was embarrassed or shamed. But the person who had heard the tape had concluded that I had meant to embarrass them.

I was really shaken. I couldn't even explain myself, since the letter writer had not signed his name.

It taught me a lesson on how careful one has to be in these matters — especially with tape recordings. I am sure the letter writer meant well, but things can be so easily taken out of context.

This is one of the meanings of the Talmudic dictum "And your eyes shall see your teachers." One should always endeavor to hear the words directly from the teacher. When something is repeated in the teacher's name, it can easily be misinterpreted, since the tone and nuance are lost.

Unfortunately, there is a limit to what you can do about this. If you're allowing a *shiur* to be recorded, you cannot constantly be thinking of how you sound on the tape. You must deliver it in your natural style. Anything else will sound awkward and insincere.

The Name Is Kaplan...David Kaplan

A regular feature of my job is traveling. It has its pros and cons, like most things in life, but one thing I love about traveling is getting the opportunity to observe people whom I would never otherwise get to meet. I've learned a lot about human nature while on the road.

On one trip home from California, I was to leave from Bradley Airport on United Airlines, stop off in Frankfurt, Germany, and then continue on to Eretz Yisrael with El Al. Like many Jews, I had a queasy feeling about being in Germany, even for the short duration of a stopover, but it wasn't possible to change the ticket.

I called United to confirm my flight, and I was told that I would actually be flying on Lufthansa, the German national airline, since they had a code-sharing agreement with United.

Oh, great, I thought. *I'll probably be the only Jew on the airplane. And I'm pretty recognizable as a Jew to boot.*

I wasn't frightened exactly, but I sure didn't feel comfortable about it.

I arrived at the Lufthansa counter to find it teeming with Germans. Not another Jew in sight. My black hat and suit earned me a lot of stares, some curious, some bordering on hostile. I actually enjoyed the attention. *Stare long and stare hard,* I mused. *We're still around, and we'll always be around.*

When I presented my ticket to the agent, she punched in a few details on her keyboard and then said, "Just a moment, sir. I must speak to my supervisor."

She walked over to an ominous-looking man and conferred with him, both of them constantly looking over at me.

After three conferences and as many trips to the computer, she handed me my ticket and said, "Okay, sir, it's been cleared."

"What was the problem? That's a perfectly valid ticket." I said this with more annoyance in my voice than I actually felt, just to let them know we will not tolerate unfair behavior.

"Oh, we happen to have two passengers with the same name on the flight, and we didn't want to mix up the bags."

"You mean there's another David Kaplan on this flight?"

"Yes, sir."

I was delighted. Not only was there another Jew, but there was another me. At least, theat's how I pictured him. After all, how on earth could he possibly look like anybody else?

The boarding went smoothly, and I found my seat on the plane, still not having identified anyone who looked even remotely Jewish.

Soon after the seatbelt sign was turned on, I heard an announcement.

"Will the passenger named David Kaplan please identify himself to the nearest flight attendant?"

Well, this should be fun, I thought. *Who do they want this time?*

It turned out that they wanted both of us in order to be certain we had the correct baggage-claim tickets.

The other David Kaplan turned out to be a tall, distinguished-looking Israeli gentleman, not religious, and not really very Jewish-looking either. He also seemed to be annoyed about something, maybe the mix-up with our names.

He asked me where I was from and how I came to be on this particular flight. I told him that I had been transferred by the airline and asked him why he wasn't flying El Al.

He said curtly, "Lufthansa is cheaper."

I asked him what he did for a living, and he told me he was a building contractor. *That's odd*, I thought. *Contractors usually make a lot of money. This guy looks successful, yet he's flying Lufthansa to save a few bucks. Where's the national pride in Israel's own airline?* Something didn't add up.

I said, "I hope they don't mix up our meals. I ordered special kosher. Did you order the regular kosher?"

"No, I don't eat kosher!" he snapped.

Suddenly it all made sense. This fellow wasn't happy to see me at all. The reason he avoided El Al was so he wouldn't have to mix with people who looked like me. His annoyance was because he had been mistaken for an Orthodox Jew. What a mortifying experience for him.

The irony was beautiful. I had been uncomfortable because there weren't any other Jews. The other David Kaplan was uncomfortable for the precise opposite reason — because there was another Jew.

I felt like telling him what I had been thinking earlier at check-in: *Sorry to disappoint you, my friend, but we're still here, and we always will be.*

I've thought about this experience a number of times. That a Jew doesn't keep kosher is unfortunately no great shock. But in front of *them*? On the German airline? Do you have so little pride in your Jewishness that you are willing to announce in front of the world, "You won — we have become just like you"?

Rabbi Mendel Weinbach tells a similar story. Two Israelis were traveling through Scotland and stopped at a non-kosher restaurant for lunch. The proprietor brought them their meals, but couldn't help watching them as they ate. Finally, unable to hold back, he approached them and said, "I'm sorry for intruding, but do you mean to tell me that your people have suffered for two thousand years just so you could eat the same food that we do?"

When the Good Guys Wear Black

Davey Breuer once provided me with an interesting perspective on being religious. I have always been extremely impressed with the sacrifices made by *ba'alei teshuvah* in becoming religious and by their willingness to give up the pleasures of society in their pursuit of spirituality. In fact, we've devoted an entire section of this book to that subject (see "The Real Heroes"). Well, one day in class, I made mention of my admiration in a very complimentary way, and I was stunned to hear from Davey, "Rabbi, you don't know what you're talking about!"

"Excuse me, Davey, did I hear you right?"

"You sure did, Rabbi! You see, you Orthodox guys have never been out there 'enjoying' all the world's pleasures, so you think you must be missing something really great. Yet you still remain religious, even though you're convinced you're missing all that fun. Now that's really difficult.

"But we BT's, we've been out there, and we know we're not really sacrificing all that much. We know we're gaining so much more from Judaism than we're giving up, so it's not all that tough.

"So if anyone's a hero, it's the *frum* guy who stays *frum!*"

I just sat there, not knowing what to say, while the rest of the class nodded their heads in agreement. Once again, I had learned something unexpected from my students.

Under the Influence

UNDER THE INFLUENCE

I find it difficult to set down an exact primer for how to bring a person close to *Yiddishkeit*. People are so different, personalities are so individual and diverse, that what may attract one person to *Yiddishkeit* might easily drive another person away. There are certain people who are actively searching for answers, while others are having a fine old time, not lacking anything, until they stumble on Judaism and find out there's more to life than they ever imagined.

So it is virtually impossible to construct one single paradigm with which to interest nonreligious Jews in Judaism. There are, however, certain rules that I have found generally hold true.

One: Be real. Be yourself. Don't put on a show for the next person. The show won't hold up when he gets to know you better, and you will look like a hypocrite.

Also, don't try to anticipate how this person perceives you as an Orthodox Jew and then try to live up to his presumptions. You will come across as insincere. Just be yourself, and you will be respected for what you are.

Another key point to remember is this: Avoid attacking the other person's beliefs or philosophies. For one thing, it's rude. For another, it's unproductive. No one likes to be confronted, especially not on such personal matters as faith and religion. You will only cause an argument, with nothing gained.

And make no mistake. The fact that you may be right is insignificant; if you make it personal, you will get nowhere. No one likes to be beaten over the head with his errors, so though you may win the argument, you won't win any friends. Intellectual integrity is fine in theory, but in reality, winning friends is far more effective. If you don't believe me, ask Dale Carnegie.

If you are in a situation where you must confront another person's belief structure, you should try to employ what is called the "Straw Man" approach. This means you create a hypothetical person or situation, a straw man mirroring your situation, and set up that straw man for the disagreement. Then it's the fictional character you've created who gets slammed for his philosophy, and your friend can laugh along with you instead of feeling threatened by your reasoning.

It may sound simplistic, but it really works.

On a related note: Any experienced *kiruv* person will tell you that very few people become *frum* only because they become convinced of the intellectual truth of the Torah. Most *ba'alei teshuvah* are attracted because they see the sanity and the beauty of the Torah lifestyle, having themselves come from a world that is pretty insane. Thus, instead of beating people over the head with didactic arguments, you must listen to and show respect for their viewpoint, and then they will hear you out. One has to overcome the desire to show them how wrong they are. This cannot be emphasized enough.

Sometimes no approach at all is necessary. A person can be positively influenced without intention.

Rabbi Michael Farber was studying in the office of his Dallas shul when there was a knock on the door.

"Come in."

A well-dressed man in his forties entered the room.

"Hello, Rabbi. My name is Fred Fisher, and I would like to make a donation to your synagogue."

"Certainly," stammered the rabbi, not used to people walking in off the street with donations. "Please sit down and tell me why you wish to help the shul."

Mr. Fisher sat down and told the following story.

"I'm Jewish, Rabbi, but I've never been very religious. I'm officially Conservative, but not very involved there either. Recently our temple organized a trip to Israel to show solidarity with our Israeli brethren, and I decided to go along. I'd never been to Israel before, and it was a real eye-opener for me.

"But the highlight of the trip was when we visited the Western Wall. I prayed and felt some closeness to God, but what was really amazing was this Hasidic Jew who was praying at the Wall. I've never seen anything like it. He prayed with such devotion, such concentration; he was oblivious to the world. I couldn't take my eyes off him. For twenty minutes I stood there and watched this Jew pray. It was like I had been given a glimpse into a world of spirituality, a world I'd never even known existed.

"Eventually I had to leave, since our bus was going, but I couldn't stop thinking about what I had seen. Those twenty minutes were the high point of my trip.

"I decided that when I returned to Dallas I would do something good in honor of the anonymous Jew I'd seen praying at the Western Wall. I wanted to make a donation to a Hasidic synagogue, but there are none in Dallas. So I called a friend and asked him which stream of Judaism would a Hasidic Jew be most closely affiliated with, Reform, Conservative, or Orthodox. He said definitely Orthodox.

"So here I am, Rabbi. I would like to donate twelve thousand dollars to your synagogue in honor of this Hasidic Jew."

Rabbi Farber was almost overcome by this amazing story. He said, "Mr. Fisher, you should know that we've had plans to build an educational wing for the shul for some time now, but we haven't had the money to get the project off the ground. Your twelve thousand dollars will help us get started on the new wing, and once we get started, it should be much easier to raise the rest of the money."

I first read this story in one of Rabbi Paysach Krohn's books, and it taught me about the tremendous influence one can have on others, not only when trying to influence them, but even when unaware that they are observing at all. It is an awesome responsibility, as well as an awesome opportunity.

The devout chassid davening in Jerusalem had no idea anyone was observing him, and he certainly never imagined that as a result of his prayer a shul in Dallas would build an educational wing, where hundreds, if not thousands, of people would learn Torah. And this chassid would have a share in every word of Torah learned in that building.

Awesome.

Not long after reading the story, I was asked to make a fund-raising appeal at a local shul, and as part of my presentation, I told this story. It made a strong impact on the audience, and the next week someone who had been at the appeal repeated it at another fund-raising event. After he finished his narrative, a young *kollel* fellow in the back approached him and said, "I know that shul. I know that story. I'm from Dallas, and my Jewish education began in that educational wing."

I'm not sure what this *yungerman*'s background is, but I know that he is a *talmid chacham* with a beautiful family. Once again, the credit is shared by the anonymous chassid who prayed at the Kosel.

Awesome.

Finally...a Winner at Wrigley

Joe Winston was paying his way through college by vending at Wrigley Field, selling hot dogs, beer, ice cream, and game programs. He made friends with some of the other vendors, among them a few Orthodox Jews.

After a while, Joe noticed that after the sixth inning of every ball game, during the break known as the seventh-inning stretch, the religious guys would disappear into the storage area for five minutes and reappear as the game got back underway.

No one ever asked him to join; they likely didn't even know that Joe was Jewish. He was curious, though, so one day he followed them in and saw that they each prayed silently for a few minutes, then recited a short communal prayer and went back to work.

Joe was pretty surprised by this. They seemed to be such normal, regular guys, not at all fanatical. He would never have guessed that they could be so responsible about something like prayer. All the other Jews he had ever known were Reform or Conservative, and he'd never seen any of them take their religious obligations so seriously.

Intrigued, he continued watching them and was amazed at their consistency and dedication to their religion. He decided he had to find the source of this steady devotion. He looked around for material on Orthodox Judaism and started attending an occasional class on Talmud and Judaism.

Despite his growing fascination, Joe found it hard to make time for his religious investigations, since he had a pretty busy schedule between college, work, and recreation. As a lifelong skeptic, he also wasn't completely convinced that this way of life was for real. But one day the final proof came.

It was a jam-packed Sunday afternoon game, with close to fifty thousand people in the stands. One of the religious vendors returned to the vending station and suddenly realized that he had been overpaid by ninety-eight dollars. He had no idea who had given him the extra money, nor was anyone coming to claim it, and the other vendors told him to just forget it and pocket the money. He'd never find the customer.

Joe didn't say anything. He just watched closely out of the corner of his eye.

Without a moment's hesitation, the Orthodox kid said, "What? Are you joking? I can't take this money. It doesn't belong to me." He insisted on retracing his steps through the crowd, asking every person in his section if the money was his, until he found the correct patron and returned the money.

That was enough proof for Joe. He knew now that Torah was for real.

Today Joe Winston is *frum* and has a regular *chavrusa* in the Lakewood Kollel in Chicago.

(Rabbi Meisels wanted to entitle this story "White Sox and Black Hats" — he overlooked the fact that the White Sox are unwelcome in this part of town.)

The Ringmaster Returns

One never knows how a single word can help (or hurt) way down the line. Sometimes an innocent remark or a friendly gesture may be the thing that turns a person toward the path of Torah.

I was standing outside the yeshivah one day when a bearded fellow approached. I didn't know him, but I nodded hello.

He walked right up to me and grabbed my hand. "Rabbi, don't you recognize me?"

"Uh, no..."

"I'm Tuvia Adams!"

Then it dawned on me. I mentally replaced the *peyos* with earrings, the mustache with a nose ring, and the black hat with a bandanna, and I was looking at Tony, the guy we used to call the "Lord of the Rings."

During Tony's first visit in yeshivah nothing happened; he came and left with more jewelry than King Tut. Now, five years later, Tuvia had returned with a wife, two kids, a long beard, and "Hi, remember me?"

I don't know what it was that got to him, whether it was a friendly word, a timely pat on the back, or an insight in a Gemara *shiur*, nor whether it was me, a fellow staff member, a student, or a family he'd visited for Shabbos, but obviously something had had an effect. Now he was Tuvia, a fulfilled, happily married young man, well on his way to becoming a *talmid chacham*.

The Heights of Courage

Sometimes the best way to get a viewpoint across is outside the classroom. Lessons are fine, but real life can be more, well, real.

I often accompany the students on the trips they take around Israel.

It is a good way to get to know the boys and see them outside their regular setting. Often a young man will open up more outdoors, in an informal setting, than in the classroom or *beis midrash*.

One summer we went mountain-climbing in the north of Israel. I was well prepared for the adventure, with my black pants, white shirt, and ancient Chicago Cubs baseball cap. I wanted to ensure that the Cubs would finally get to the top of something.

After some serious huffing and puffing, we reached the first peak, whereupon I became cognizant of a rather prosaic, but never so terrifyingly imminent truism: what goes up must come down. All my life I have been terrified of heights, and now I was peering at this yawning chasm, with nothing but a weather-beaten guide rope and my rapidly dwindling courage to help me down.

I let the boys go first, explaining that I would bring up the rear to make sure everyone got down safely.

With their ever-vigilant rebbe keeping an eye on them, the guys went merrily springing down the cliff, until I was the only one left. Realizing that I had a choice between staying up there forever and perhaps becoming a Tibetan monk or following my charges down the rocks, I opted for the latter and gingerly picked my way down to terra firma.

When we got to the second mountain, I remembered the cliché about the things that go up having to come down and said, "No, thanks, guys, I'll pass. I'll just walk around this mountain instead of climbing it."

Afterward, when I met them on the other side, Alan Waxman approached me and asked, in a voice loud enough for everyone to hear, "Rabbi, why didn't you come up the mountain?"

"I'll tell you the truth, Alan. I'm terrified of heights."

"But, Rabbi, don't you think overcoming that fear and climbing the mountain would display true courage?"

I smiled at him. "No, Alan, true courage is to be able to look up at all thirty of you and say, 'I'm too scared to do that.' "

The point hit home. True courage is to be able to look around at society and say, "I've got convictions, and despite the peer pressure, I'm not going to give in."

Of course, I was really just too chicken to climb the mountain — but I thought the metaphor was good.

I wasn't so lucky when we went to the water park. There was a very, very fast slide at this park, and I was having a good time watching the boys speed down and hit the water with a titanic splash. But they kept saying, "Let's go, Rebbe. Are you chicken?" and "Don't worry, Rebs. You'll probably be okay."

Finally, unable to withstand the pressure, I slowly ascended the seemingly endless staircase, all the while hoping it would start raining or something. No such luck. My pride had compelled me to do for free something that ten minutes earlier I wouldn't have done for money.

I did it. I should have come up with another metaphor.

The Vital Spark of Yiddishkeit

The Gemara talks about Rabbi Elazar ben Dordaya, a prototype *ba'al teshuvah*. He was a man who sank to the depths of depravity, and from those very depths he was inspired and began on his trek toward full repentance. It is not a path that is necessarily encouraged, but it does serve to remind us that almost anything can spur a particular person to rethink his direction in life.

Shauli Moskowitz might be called a modern-day Rabbi Elazar ben Dordaya. When Shauli first came to the yeshivah, he had long hair, an earring, and a real desire to learn Torah. A yeshivah high school graduate from a very affluent family, Shauli had been off the *derech* for a while and was now on his way back.

One evening I said, "Tell me, Shauli, what brought you back? What made you come to the yeshivah?"

"Well, I was at a disco one night, and I took a look around at the people I was associating with, at my so-called friends, and at the things that I was doing. I couldn't believe the depths to which I had sunk. I was basically an animal on two legs. At that moment I said to myself, *This is ridiculous.* I decided that I was going to fast, which I did for an entire day. Then I put on tefillin for the first time in years and davened, and I actually felt a rejuvenation of my spirit. Soon after I broke up with my girlfriend and started learning a little Torah. Finally I decided that the only way to do it right was to come to Eretz Yisrael and learn full-time in a yeshivah. So here I am."

Shauli stayed in the yeshivah for about half a year, and today he is learning full-time in a yeshivah in the United States.

You never know when it will kick in, but there is always that spark in a Jew's soul that, in the most unlikely circumstances, can suddenly, unexpectedly, burst into flame.

"You Shall Not Stumble"

In the library of Hebrew University in Jerusalem, there is an extensive collection of rare manuscripts and microfilms of many hard-to-find documents and *sefarim*.

One day a young yeshivah student was doing research there on a certain old manuscript. After several hours of study, he felt hungry, so he found a quiet corner, pulled out a sandwich, and ate. Upon finishing his lunch, he realized he did not have a siddur, so he *bentched* by heart, closing his eyes so he could concentrate better. As he finished, he noticed the librarian — a young nonreligious woman — standing above him and shaking her head.

"I noticed you said the words *'v'lo nikashel'* (and we shall not stumble). I can assure you that there is no source for adding those words to the prayer. I myself am from a traditional home and have never come across that wording, nor have I ever seen it in any prayer book."

The boy was very surprised. She didn't look as though she knew what *bentching* was, let alone have opinions on the proper wording. But he merely said, "You are making a mistake. It is true that those words are not in all siddurim, but it is a custom in some communities, and that is why I said it."

She did not agree, and they argued about it for a few minutes, until he said, "Look, I'll go home tonight and make a copy of that page in my siddur where those words appear, and I will send you the copy. Okay?"

She agreed, and that ended the discussion.

When he got home, he forgot his promise to the librarian. When he did remember the discussion, it was always inconvenient to make the copy. Several months went by. Finally, he decided that he had better make good on his word, and he photocopied the appropriate page, circled the words *"v'lo nikashel"* with a red marker, and mailed it off. He never received a reply from the girl, and to his mind, that was the end of that.

Two years later he was living in Bnei Brak, and he received an invitation in the mail one day. It was to a wedding in Ramat Gan, a nearby suburb. He was very puzzled; he did not recognize the name of the groom or bride. His wife didn't know them either. The young man figured it must be a mistake, probably because of his rather common name, and he decided that he would not attend the wedding.

As it happened, on the night of the wedding he was in the neighborhood where the wedding was taking place, and he decided to drop in. He entered the wedding hall, took one look around and realized that indeed he knew no one, and turned to leave. As he did so, he felt a tap on the shoulder.

"Excuse me, are you Chaim Cohen?"

"Yes, I am."

"The bride would like to speak with you."

"Who is the bride? I shouldn't even be here."

"Just come with me."

Chaim walked over to the head table and said to the *chasan* and *kallah*, "Mazel tov."

"Do you recognize me?" asked the *kallah*.

"Um, no. Have we met?"

"Yes. I was a librarian at Hebrew University two years ago. We had a discussion one day about the proper wording of *bentching*. At the time, I was going out with an Arab boy, and he really wanted me to marry him. I couldn't decide and kept pushing off my answer. Finally, he gave an ultimatum: either I marry him or it was over. I decided to say yes and arranged to meet him at a coffee shop for lunch, where we would get engaged. As I was leaving my apartment, the mail arrived. Someone had sent me a photocopied page of an old prayer book. The words '*v'lo nikashel*,' circled in red, jumped out at me.

"I thought, *Someone is trying to tell me something*. I dumped Ahmed, began attending a seminary for *ba'alei teshuvah*, and tonight I am marrying a man who plans to spend his life involved in Torah learning and teaching. And it is all thanks to you."

To Light a Candle

The following story comes from Rabbi Paysach Krohn, and I've used it many times to illustrate the power of a well-timed word.

At a convention in Ashdod for Israeli *ba'alei teshuvah*, a young woman stood up and related the story of her family's return to *Yiddishkeit*.

She and her husband were happily married, with a new baby girl, when they decided to purchase an apartment. Not being wealthy, and wishing to remain within commuting distance of their jobs, they were somewhat limited in choice of neighborhoods.

They wound up in a middle-class area on the outskirts of Bnei Brak, which is a rather religious neighborhood. But this did not affect them much, since their immediate surroundings were less observant, ranging from completely nonreligious to somewhat traditional.

They were quite happy with their situation, their neighbors, and their darling daughter, Anat, who had since been joined by a little brother, Yarden.

When the time came to send Anat to school, the family encountered their first dilemma. The most convenient primary school for their schedules and location was a school in Bnei Brak, the aforementioned religious enclave. They did not want their daughter educated by backward religious fanatics. But any other arrangement would be extremely difficult to coordinate with their busy schedules.

With great misgivings, they decided to pay a visit to the school and see if it was at all compatible with their needs. They were hoping that the school would reject them because of their secular lifestyle, and then the decision would be taken out of their hands.

This was not the case. The school was very accepting of their daughter and willing to have her join as long as she conformed to school rules while there. The parents were also pleasantly surprised to find the principal and teacher to be worldly, nonfanatical people who were clearly interested in providing a warm and loving educational environment for the children.

Walking home, they decided they would enroll Anat in this school, while keeping an eye out for undue religious coercion. In any case, once she reached the third or fourth grade, they would transfer her to a school better suited to their lifestyle.

Things went along swimmingly for a while. Anat would bring home her arts and crafts and proudly show them to her parents, telling them about the various festivals and Jewish occasions. Harmless stuff.

The second year she began learning the *alef-beis*, which every Israeli child learns, and both parents were sure they had made the right decision.

One day Anat came home and said, "Ima, can you start covering your hair?" She had apparently learned that married Jewish women are supposed to cover their hair in public and wanted her mommy to be like everyone else.

Ima said, "I'm sorry, Anat. That's not our way of life," and the matter was dropped.

Sometime later, Anat had another request. "Ima, can we have only kosher food in the house?" Again her mother patiently explained to her that this was not their way, and while it was fine for some people, it wasn't really necessary.

By the time Anat asked if they could light Shabbos candles, Ima's patience was wearing a little thin, and she snapped, "No, Anat, and stop bothering me with these religious *shtuyot*."

Feeling chastised, Anat crept out of the kitchen and went up to her own bedroom. However, being a spunky kid, she soon went outside and walked down the block to the grocery store.

"Hi, Motty, can you give me two candles? Ima needs them for Shabbat."

Motty knew the family. He knew they weren't religious and couldn't possibly need Shabbos candles. He decided that she must really want *yahrtzeit* candles, which are lit on the anniversary of the death of a loved one and which even many nonreligious Israelis light.

Anat took the candles and skipped home. She found matches in the kitchen and brought them to her room, where she set up the candles on the windowsill, made the blessing as her teacher had taught her, and lit them.

In the meantime, her mother had grown a little concerned. Anat had been in her room for a long time, and her mother felt guilty for having snapped at her earlier. After all, they had sent Anat to a religious school, so she couldn't be blamed for wanting to practice what she learned.

She climbed the steps to Anat's room, opened the door, and saw her little daughter sitting on the floor, gazing raptly at the two *yahrtzeit* flames burning brightly.

"Anat, what are you doing?"

The child jumped to her feet, caught red-handed.

"Ima, please don't be angry. One is for you, and one is for Daddy."

Her mother stopped short. She had been ready to yell at Anat for disobeying her, for lighting a fire in the house, when the full import of her child's words struck her.

These were *yahrtzeit* candles, which signify a dead person, and "one is for you, and one is for Daddy."

At that moment she said to herself, *You know, maybe we are dead inside. Maybe our life is missing some vital spark. We've been doing our best to avoid any kind of spiritual contact, but perhaps this is God's way of reminding us that we aren't fully alive, and we need yahrtzeit candles lit for us.*

"This is my story," said the woman, "and thanks to God and Anat, I and my family are now truly alive."

Holy Is as Holy Does

Many professional *kiruv* workers assert that nowadays it is self-defeating to give strong rebuke because all it will do is backfire. People are very sensitive and defensive, and in order to be effective one must use a gentle, nonaccusatory approach.

Guilt is out.

A certain rabbi with whom I am acquainted was on a panel addressing an audience of about two hundred. Many of the attendees were parents of *ba'alei teshuvah*, and several had an ax to grind.

One mother stood up and said, "Ever since my daughter has become religious, she projects a holier-than-thou attitude. What do you say about that, gentlemen? Is that what you teach them to do?"

The first respondent stood up and said very apologetically, "Of course not. We don't teach these kids to have such an attitude. On the contrary, we try to encourage them to respect their parents and siblings and not to push their religion in anyone's face."

The next rabbi said pretty much the same thing, and so on down the line. All the while the inquisitor was standing and nodding grimly, with a thoroughly vindicated expression on her face.

My friend was the last speaker of the night. When he got up, he looked straight at the woman and said, "Madam, may I ask you a question? Has the thought ever crossed your mind that maybe your daughter *is* holier than you?

"When is the last time you thought about your relationship with God? When is the last time you prayed sincerely and with devotion? When is the last time you did some self-examination, some self-introspection?"

There went her self-satisfied smirk.

The rabbi was later told that this lady said she hated him for saying this to her. While this didn't come to him as much of a surprise, he felt badly that she was insulted.

But at the same time, he believed that he had done the correct thing. He couldn't let everyone leave that evening with the thought that, yes, people who become *ba'alei teshuvah* make their parents uncomfortable and are rude and inconsiderate, while their parents are paragons of courtesy.

Whether or not the approach was justified, I can't say for sure. I wasn't there. But it is certainly true that under certain circumstances specialized approaches may be necessary.

The Aura of a Great Man

On one class trip we took the boys to Bnei Brak to meet some of the great *gedolim* of the generation. One of the sages we went to visit was Rav Chaim Kanievsky, *shlita*. Rav Chaim is a great sage and tzaddik and is particularly famous for his incredible diligence in learning, quite literally never wasting a second.

Wisely, we made an appointment in advance and were ushered right in. As we entered, Rav Chaim looked up from his *sefer* and saw that the guys were still filing in, so he put his head back down to his usual position and continued studying. When everyone was in the room, he stopped his studying for a minute, looked at the boys, and gave them all a very warm *berachah*.

We stayed and watched him for a couple of minutes, and then everyone filed out. Once out of the room I walked over to Arthur Luke, and said, "So, Art, what did you think?"

Granted, Art is an effusive type, but he looked at me and said with a lot of emotion, "Rabbi, I can't tell you what it was, but he was exuding something."

Such is the strength of Torah.

Leave Off with the Sports, Rabbi

Many successful *kiruv* workers like to share their general knowledge with people to show that they're not closed off to the world. This helps to combat the impression that people have of rabbis as closeted, insular fanatics. So if they know any fascinating tidbits about zoology or entomology, they like to show it off.

My expertise is sports, and I always like to use it as an icebreaker. If a kid comes from Alabama, I say something about Bear Bryant or Joe Namath a.k.a. Broadway Joe. If he's from Boston, I can talk about Larry Bird or the Green Monster in Fenway. And if I'm ever stuck for a local athlete, then I just bring up Michael Jordan. You can discuss him with a Confucian scholar.

It's really a great icebreaker, first of all because it gives me something to discuss with a complete stranger and also because it breaks the stereotype of black-bearded rabbis.

One time a young man from Seattle happened into the office.

"Hi, there. What's your name?" I inquired.

"Hello, Rabbi, my name is Bert. I'm from Seattle."

"Wow, Seattle, you must be a Sonics fan."

"Well...no, actually, I think that following sports is rather inane."

"Oh! Yeah, me, too, so do I."

I guess that guy called for some entomology.

Convicts with Conviction

There is an organization here in Israel that runs prison *kiruv* programs. It introduces Torah and Jewish life to some of the roughest elements in the prison population. Those prisoners who show a sincere interest in self-improvement and religious observance over a significant period of time receive consideration from the authorities for early release.

The criticism of such programs, of course, is that anyone can put on a *kippah* and claim to be religious. In order to determine the efficacy of the program, and in light of the anti-religious sentiment surrounding it, the prison authorities did a study of the relative rates of recidivism.

They found that releasees from prison had a recidivism rate of 70 percent. Those released because of renewed religious conviction had a recidivism rate of only 6 percent. The program was shown to be so successful that the Israeli government even got involved in funding it. They probably figured that as bad as religious Jews are for society, criminals are even worse.

Of course, Achad Ha'am, the famous Zionist, probably wasn't very happy. As he notably said, he couldn't wait for Israel to have its very own prisons and prisoners.

Not so sympathetic was the *Jerusalem Post*. They presented a list of twenty-five ways to improve Jerusalem. Suggestion number nine was that "all yeshivah students and convicts" should be kept busy sweeping the streets.

When I saw this, I was shocked beyond belief. How did that suggestion find itself all the way down at number nine?

The next thing you know, the other Jewish "religious" movements will also want such a program. Of course, the prisoners won't have to actually do any mitzvos or even profess any belief in God. They just have to call themselves good Jews and maybe pay dues at a temple. We'll call it "The Egalitarian Release Program — Everyone Goes!"

Who Makes the Cholent in the House?

Robert Brooks was a different kind of challenge. He felt he had to disagree with every Torah value just on principle. Sometimes his arguments seemed more emotional than logical, as though there were something driving him beyond the actual discussion at hand.

Among the causes Robert embraced, at least in the classroom, was feminism. One day he wouldn't leave me alone, challenging everything I said, so I slowly warmed up with some snide remarks about equality. Everyone laughed, including Robert; he knew I was just trying to bait him.

Finally I told him a story.

Two young girls went to see HaRav Shach, *zt"l*, the *gadol hador*, and asked him to explain a very difficult passage in the *Ramban*, a preeminent Torah commentator.

Rav Shach waited till they had articulated their difficulty and then smiled and said, "My wife also doesn't understand that *Ramban*, but she makes a delicious cholent. Go home and learn how to make cholent."

His point was that study for women is commendable, and there is a place for it, but this was not the place. He recognized that these were two *frum* girls trying to prove a political point to the *gadol hador*, and he gently rebuked them. We do not take a position against all learning for women, but it must be guided by *gedolei Torah* and by tradition.

When I finished relating the story, Robert said to me, "Isn't that *lashon hara* on Rav Shach?"

"No, Robert, I think it's a positive story."

He looked at me incredulously. "Rabbi, does your wife know you say these things?"

"Sure!" I answered. "She agrees with me. You're welcome to call her up and ask her what she thinks."

That ended the discussion on feminism, and we resumed the *shiur*.

After lunch and a rest period, we had another scheduled Talmud class. The guys were just settling down when Robert walked in with a dejected expression on his face. I looked at him questioningly, and he just shook his head slowly and said, "Rebbe, I can't believe that there's actually another person in the world who thinks the way you do."

He had called my wife.

Robert and I became pretty close, and I later discovered that my initial feeling had been correct. Robert had siblings who had become religious, and while attracted to religion himself, he was being very careful about falling into the same trap. He wanted to be one hundred percent sure before he committed to anything.

Today Robert is religious and married to a wonderful girl, but I'm sure that he, not his wife, makes the cholent in their house.

Where's Walter?

Just as in any field of endeavor, not all ends rosily in *kiruv*. Through my years in outreach, I have been involved in some very troubling situations and witnessed a number of students undergoing genuine trials.

Walter Carfeld was the dream student. He was bright, engaging, a good conversationalist, and lively in the classroom. He loved to shmooze, and he told me marvelous, entertaining stories, quite a few of which centered on his father, a multimillionaire with his own private parking spot at the Beverly Hills Synagogue, the wealthiest synagogue in the world.

Looking for some excitement after his privileged childhood, Walter had joined the Marines, where he had some truly amazing adventures as he traveled the world.

Eventually, however, even that excitement palled, and Walter made his way to Kfar Chabad, a Lubavitch enclave, in search of new excitement. There he started becoming observant, and after some more interesting adventures, Walter came to a yeshivah with which I was affiliated. He learned well, behaved himself, and kept everyone entertained with his varied reminiscences. It seemed as though the perpetual thrill-seeker had finally found his ultimate thrill — being an observant, Torah-studying Jew.

One day Walter didn't come to the regular *shiur*. I wasn't concerned. Occasionally things come up, and a guy has to miss a class. After a couple of days' absence, however, I inquired about him in the office. What I heard absolutely blew my mind. To this day I have trouble assimilating the truth about this dream student.

It turned out that Walter had been caught stealing money and belongings from other students and had been asked to leave the yeshivah. It turned out that this was also the reason he had left Kfar Chabad. Not only that, but he was a pathological liar. He had never been in the Marines, nor anywhere else he had claimed. There was no multimillionaire father, perhaps no father at all. There wasn't even a parking spot at the synagogue in Beverly Hills.

I felt bad because Walter had such potential that I wished it all had been true. And I think about what must have driven Walter to such a state, and then I feel even worse.

Things Happen

It's hard to get through to anyone who is not willing to put in at least some effort at self-discipline.

A group of guys was staying in the yeshivah for the summer, and the fast day of 17 Tammuz was approaching. This is a very serious and sober day in the history of our nation, and the day before the fast I spoke to the class about its significance and the reason it was instituted. I encouraged them to at least try to fast.

On the eighteenth of Tammuz, I opened class with "So how'd you guys do yesterday?"

Alan said, "Well, Rabbi, it was rough, but I made it all the way."

"Great job, Alan. How about you, Kurt?"

"I really tried, Rabbi, but about halfway through I just had to have something to eat. I was fainting from hunger."

"Tom?"

"Well, you know, I really made up my mind to fast. At eleven o'clock I was walking downtown, and I passed a falafel store, and then, I just don't know, something happened."

"Something happened" is a perfect description of Tom. He is happy-go-lucky, irrepressible — and irresponsible. He's got no goals, no plans. He dropped out of college, roamed the world, and can't manage to hold down a job for more than a month. Among other nonstarters, Tom had been fired from a loading dock and a pharmacy. Something always "happened."

When he left the yeshivah, I had a talk with him. I said, "Look, Tom, I don't know what you are going to do with the rest of your life, and I don't know if you will ever be observant, but I can tell you one thing for sure. If you don't grow up and start taking some responsibility for your actions, you will never be a happy person."

Plane Talk

I was seated next to a Semitic-looking guy on a flight to Toronto. I was trying to figure out if he was Jewish and a good *kiruv* target when the stewardess came by and offered me a chicken sandwich.

I asked her if it was kosher, and she said, "No, I'm sorry, sir. We have nothing kosher on this flight."

Without waiting for a reply, she plopped it on my tray and continued on her rounds.

I was struck, as always, by the attitude outsiders have regarding religious people's commitment. They think a request for kosher is like a request for Coca-Cola — if there is none, we'll gladly take Pepsi.

I examined the sandwich for kosher certification and decided that I would have to return it. Normally I would offer it to my seatmate, but I couldn't give non-kosher food to my possibly Jewish neighbor.

The stewardess came back, and I said, "Thank you, ma'am, but this is not kosher. Please take it back."

My neighbor piped up. "Why isn't that kosher? It's chicken and chicken is kosher!"

I thought to myself, *Oh, good. A Yid. We've got forty-five minutes, and there's nowhere he can go. A nonreligious Jew stuck next to a rabbi. Now there's a tasty kosher lunch. For me Gan Eden (Paradise), for him, Gehinnom (not Paradise).*

"How do you know what kosher is? Are you Jewish?" I asked.

"Oh, I'm Egyptian. My wife is Jewish."

After recovering from this punch in the solar plexus, I asked him about his family. He told me he had two daughters, and he was raising them completely secular. He personally didn't believe in God and was indoctrinating his kids in that belief or, rather, lack of belief. But if they ever did decide to seek religion, he was willing to be supportive and wouldn't interfere with their search.

I tried to think of some positive way to touch him in the short time we had together for the sake of his daughters. For all I knew, this might be the last time he'd ever meet a religious Jew.

Finally I said to him, "Look, do your daughters a favor. If they ever do decide to pursue their Jewish roots, make sure they go to an Orthodox rabbi. It'll save them a lot of heartache."

I don't know what effect, if any, my words will ever have, but you never know. Sometimes a casual word is the one that's remembered far down the line.

Those Ultra-Orthodox!

THOSE ULTRA-ORTHODOX!

Often, in the course of interaction with the nonreligious sector, I'm confronted with various criticisms, misconceptions, and outright canards regarding the Orthodox Jewish community.

Among the topics that crop up is the confusion over the necessity of Torah study, Orthodox society, Judaism, and religion in general. Often these issues arise as innocent questions, born of misunderstanding, and as such are definitely worth clarifying for the questioner. When a person has a genuine curiosity and a willingness to learn about *Yiddishkeit*, it is our job to help him learn.

Unfortunately, more frequently what is presented as a question is really an ill-disguised attack on the Torah way of life. In such cases, it is fruitless to respond, since the questioner is just looking to bait the speaker and make him look bad in front of his audience.

As Rav Chaim of Volozhin once told a freethinker, "For you, my friend, I have no answers, because you don't have any questions; you only have answers, and to answers, there are no answers."

His point was that this person felt guilty about his secular way of life, and his so-called questions on Judaism were meant only to salve his own guilty conscience. So he didn't really have questions; he had only answers — answers for his own wrongdoings. This point still holds true today. Nonetheless, regardless of their motivation, such attacks can often create uncertainty even in religious Jews, especially if they've never thought about the issues being presented and are hearing the particular criticism for the first time.

Thus it behooves us, for our own sake, to understand the true answers to these questions and to find an effective way of dealing with these challenges. This is particularly crucial for *ba'alei teshuvah*, who are often thrown into a Torah life without the benefit of a lifetime of preparation. They must suddenly know the reasons for, and the answers to, the most complex system of living in the world.

And they don't have time to do it piecemeal — they've got parents, siblings, and business partners demanding explanations for their "irrational" behavior, and they want those answers now!

Basic concepts, such as studying Torah for its own sake, which to us are so fundamental to living, are completely foreign to the outside world. If a person is not earning a degree or learning a useful trade, why on earth would he spend ten hours a day studying archaic laws? That is one criticism with which *ba'alei teshuvah* often must contend. "Why are you still sitting in yeshivah? What good is all this learning? When are you going to do something useful with your life?"

There are many excellent books that discuss the major issues one may encounter in *kiruv*. I will just address some of those that I have run into on the job.

Doctor Do Little — Very Little!

I broke my foot once, and after limping around in a cast for several weeks, I went to the doctor to get the cast changed. The doctor was a nonreligious Jew who came from my hometown of Chicago, so naturally we ended up chatting. After the usual pleasantries, he asked me, "What do you do here in Israel?" I replied that I was learning in *kollel*.

He says, "Uh-huh. And how do you support yourself?"

"Well, my wife works."

"Hmph. Well, I guess someone has to, huh?" he said with a smirk.

I didn't respond verbally to this, of course, since he was holding my broken foot in his hands. But I thought to myself, *I can't believe you! Here you are, a doctor. Someone put you through medical school, either the*

United States government or your father or your wife. Even if you earned a full scholarship, someone other than yourself paid for your education. You obviously don't consider yourself a moocher, so why did you take their hard-earned money?

The answer is that you and the person who paid for it considered your medical education a worthy value, something worth spending a small fortune for. So you had no problem taking their hard-earned money so you could study in medical school.

Well, we feel Torah is a value. Torah study for its own sake, without the promise of monetary reward is a worthy value, and it is worthwhile spending one's hard-earned money for it. So whether we're supported by our parents or by our wife or by someone else, if they are willing to support us and they appreciate the inherent worth of Torah study, why shouldn't we learn in kollel?

If you think the study of the Amazon River basin is important and the United States government agrees, go for it. Get the grant and bring along plenty of mosquito repellent. Personally I think Torah study is important, and my own Treasury Department, otherwise known as my spouse and parents, agrees, so that's what I do.

Anyway, that's what went through my mind as I sat in the doctor's office, and now that no one's holding my broken foot, I'm free to tell you what I really think.

The Think Tank

Over the years I've heard a similar refrain from students who have become committed to *Yiddishkeit*. It's usually something along the lines of "You know, Rabbi, I like being *frum*. I like the religion, but I just can't see myself learning forever."

My standard response is "Well, frankly, neither can I. In fact, I don't know anyone who is going to live forever, let alone learn all that time."

What they mean, of course, is that they can't see themselves only studying for the rest of their lives, on a full-time basis.

In truth, I don't know many people who do actually remain in yeshivah full-time. Most of us eventually leave the *beis midrash* and find salaried employment. After all, we need some income to support our "irresponsibly" large families. It's actually ironic. Here the questioner is, talking to me about learning full-time, and I myself don't learn full-time.

I teach.

It's true that teaching provides continued incentive for one's own learning. But it is a profession like any other.

I try to explain that learning is not meant to be full-time for the majority of the population. People have a responsibility to support their families, and they have no right to demand that someone else support them while they learn. So they shouldn't worry about having to learn, as they say, forever.

But if one has the opportunity to learn full-time before financial or other pressures mandate involvement in something more active, one should definitely take advantage of the opportunity. There are certain individuals who do have the ability to continue learning full-time, both from a financial point of view and from the standpoint of gaining satisfaction and personal growth from their Torah study. These lucky few certainly should continue learning for as long as possible. After all, they have the financial and moral support to do so, so why shouldn't they learn Torah? No one would complain if they joined a Harvard think tank to study global economics or the migratory habits of mountain butterflies.

So why are they so annoyed if we learn Torah?

Man Bites Dog

Then there are the questions about Orthodox Jews who have committed crimes. How could an Orthodox Jew, someone who observes the Torah, do something so terrible?

The corollary to this question is that the Torah is bad, all Orthodox Jews are bad, and the whole system is corrupt — so why should I be a part of it?

There is a response to this from Rav Mottel Katz, *zt"l*, the *rosh yeshivah* of Telshe in Wickliffe, Ohio. When asked how he felt about an Orthodox Jew who cheats on his taxes, Reb Mottel responded, "And how do you feel about an Orthodox Jew who eats on Yom Kippur?"

His student replied, "But, Rebbe, a Jew who eats on Yom Kippur is by definition not Orthodox."

"My friend, a Jew who cheats on his taxes is also not Orthodox."

Not that Reb Mottel was equating tax evasion with eating on Yom Kippur, but he was establishing a very important truth.

Just because a man wears a certain kind of hat and lives in a particular neighborhood doesn't necessarily mean he is a representative of the entire community. A single unscrupulous individual, or even several such individuals, are not at all a picture of what *Yiddishkeit* really is, no more than a single killing makes all gentiles murderers or a single hate group turns all Southerners into racists.

This approach is not enough, though. Human nature being what it is, people do form bad impressions of a group based on the acts of an individual. And the person asking the question is usually not satisfied with this answer because what he really wants to know is how a Jew who is supposedly Orthodox could do such a thing.

There is a famous adage in Western journalism: "Dog bites man is not news; man bites dog is news."

The fact is that a *frum* Jewish criminal is a rarity, certainly concerning the baser crimes that are commonplace in America, and even in the so-called white-collar sector. Therefore, when these crimes are committed by an Orthodox person, it shows up ever so clearly on the radar.

It's news. And more than anywhere else, it's news in the Israeli news media.

I once had an opportunity to speak in an Israeli prison. The place was full of real bad guys, truly a collection worthy of Rikers Island. I took note of a lone inmate, an Orthodox Jew. He stood out from these hooligans like a very sore thumb.

"What did he do?" I asked the program coordinator.

"Him? Tax evasion."

The minute I walked in I knew he wasn't one of the hard-core criminals.

So when a *"frum"* Jew does commit a noteworthy crime, it becomes news and tends to be magnified out of all proportion.

I'm not condoning crimes, white- or blue-collar. But while it does exist among religious Jews, such misconduct should be kept in the proper perspective.

A final point on this subject: If you see a wrong being committed by a religious Jew, don't assume it is due to a flaw in the Torah; it's a flaw in that individual. His inappropriate, or even criminal, behavior is in *spite* of what the Torah says, not *because* of what the Torah says.

Looking Forward — and Not Sideways!

"Rabbi, I'm bothered by the use of a *mechitzah*."

"Yes, Ralph, what's the problem?"

"Why do we need *mechitzahs*? I think it's fanatical overkill."

"Ralph, the *mechitzah* is there to enable us to concentrate on davening."

"Rabbi, are you Orthodox really so weak-minded that you can't concentrate on davening when there are women in the room?"

"Yes, Ralph, we are weak. We understand that there are certain human weaknesses, and we must take them into account. We don't pretend they don't exist. If we have a weakness, and quite frankly this is one of mankind's greatest weaknesses, then we have an obligation to deal with it, not to pretend it doesn't exist."

"But, Rabbi, if it's to prevent a human failing, then why do only Orthodox shuls insist on a *mechitzah*? I've never seen one in a Reform or Conservative temple."

"I don't know, Ralph. I guess we Orthodox Jews are just not as morally strong as they are."

Cheaper by the Dozen

"Why do religious Jews have so many kids? Doesn't family size hamper the attention each child will get?"

When I get asked this question, I must do my utmost to avoid lashing out at the person asking the question. After all, here we have someone who was probably not given as much attention as he would have liked and needed. In many cases, the questioner comes from a divorced home, went to P.S. 912, was in class 4b, sat in a row 16, seat 3... — all his life he's been nothing but a number, and he wants to know about religious kids getting enough quality attention.

We discuss the issue and talk about how a child is a blessing, and I usually end the conversation telling him that I have a neighbor who has seven daughters.

"Seven daughters? That's unbelievable!"

"That's right, seven daughters and...nine sons."

Shocked silence.

"And, gentlemen, I can tell you that every one of them thinks of himself as an only child."

Sometimes the debate goes on.

"But the world doesn't have enough resources for all these people."

"First of all, Peter, that is simply not true. There are plenty of resources in the world. They just have to be distributed more efficiently. We are nowhere near depleting the world's resources."

"Yeah, maybe, but these people can't support their families."

"Also not quite true. Some can and some can't. But that is something that's true throughout the world, even among people who have small families."

"But don't you think it's wrong to bring so many kids into the world? You can't give them the individual attention they need."

"Frankly, Peter, my experience has been that parents who can give attention to two children can give attention to ten children, while parents who don't have enough time for ten children won't have enough time for two children either. It's just a matter of priorities."

"Okay, but, Rabbi, let's be practical. How can a mom divide her love among so many?"

"To quote one mother's answer to this question, she doesn't divide — she multiplies. It's all in the attitude. If you believe that the children you've brought into the world are part of yourself and are a major part of your life's accomplishment, then you won't shortchange them on the attention."

"What if a mother wants to work? Isn't child-rearing going to inhibit her ability to join the workforce?"

"That's an excellent point, Peter, and as a matter of fact, it might do just that. Which is why many *frum* women don't work outside the home. They consider child-rearing their primary occupation. Of course, if a mother can work outside the home without compromising her domestic devotion, there's obviously nothing wrong with it."

"Rabbi, let me tell you, if I was Orthodox, I wouldn't want to keep this law. Two kids and a dog is plenty for me!"

"Peter, we're talking about people whose belief in their system is axiomatic. That's what Torah Judaism is. One of our life goals and obligations is to populate the world so that more people can serve God. We accept this, just as we accept all the mitzvos.

"And we are very happy with it, and we make it work."

This is not just a way of deflecting criticism; it is quite literally true. In America, where the average family has about 1.3 children, we don't stop hearing about how both parents have to work in order to make ends meet. This leads to troubles — latchkey children and complaints about how no one has spare time for anything anymore, including family activities.

If small families are the solution to financial difficulty, then why must both parents work in America? It's obvious that the greater cause of economic privation is American consumerism, not the size of the family.

Trimming the Roster

I once suggested to a student of mine a novel method of dealing with this criticism.

His mother-in-law, in most respects a wonderful lady and a loving grandmother, could not make peace with his having so many kids. She was constantly nagging him about the burden on his wife, on society, on each individual child, and so on, and it was driving him batty.

He came to me for advice, and I told him about a method I'd been told was very effective. He should line up all of his kids, adorable children all, and ask his mother-in-law, "Okay, Mom, here they are — Chaim, Ahuva, Ari, Tamar, Yossi, and Esther. Now which one of them should we not have had?"

He never heard another word on the subject.

A Relentless Headache

I was sitting in a doctor's waiting room reviewing the weekly parashah. About twenty feet away from me sat a nonreligious woman who looked to be in her thirties.

I was whispering the text of what I was learning, and after about a minute she turned to me and said, "Hush! This isn't a shul, Rabbi. You're giving me a headache."

Very respectfully I said, "Sorry, I didn't mean to bother you."

I had been murmuring so quietly that I knew it couldn't have been the noise that bothered her. I wondered, if I had been whispering the words of a magazine article or a children's book, would she have minded? Rather than make a fuss, though, I just let it go and continued learning in silence.

She had the appointment before mine, and when she left the doctor's office, I went in. I said to the doctor, "The lady who was just here was giving me a bad time out there. What do you think her problem is?"

This doctor himself was an observant man. He looked at me and chuckled. "Well, she's married to a German goy, and I'm pretty certain that had something to do with it."

When one's husband is a goy, her conscience doesn't permit her any rest, and she is disturbed by any reminders of her Jewishness.

Whaddya Mean, What Do I Mean?

Often people are put on the defensive due to the use of some undefined term. You get hit with some generalized canard and don't know how to respond to it. If you get the attacker to define what he means, you'll see that there was usually no substance to the attack.

Sid Fishman asked me a very interesting question. "Rabbi, are we against the government? Do we oppose the State of Israel?"

I said, "What do you mean?"

He looked at me with a puzzled expression and said, "I mean, are we against the state?"

"What do you mean?"

Sid was getting frustrated. "Rabbi, I was sitting at a Shabbos table, and there were guys there from a Zionist yeshivah. They said to me that we are against the state. So now I'm asking you, are we against the state?"

I said, "Whenever anyone accuses you of something, or attacks you for a religious reason, always make him define what he means. Don't panic and assume he knows what he's talking about. Make him explain himself.

"What do they mean when they say we are against the state? Does it mean that we refuse to live in Israel? If it does, then I haven't been anti-Israel for the last fourteen years.

"Does it mean we burn the Israeli flag? Do we avoid paying taxes? No, we don't.

"I would say a person who is anti-government is someone who actively protests government policy and government decisions, such as those concerning land for peace and other policies. In fact, there has been talk of a general insubordination in the army ranks. So you see, it all depends on how you define 'anti-Israel.'

"Don't assume that the questioner is making a valid point. Make him clarify what he is asking, and you will find that he is often just spouting a cliché he doesn't even understand."

The next day, during Gemara *shiur*, I asked the class a question on the section we were studying. "Is this proof a final proof or not?"

Sid Fishman said immediately, "Define 'final proof.' " He was kidding, but I could tell he had understood the previous day's lesson.

This is not to say that one should dissemble or try to pull the wool over anyone's eyes. I have no qualms admitting that I have an ideological problem with the modus operandi of the government of Israel and its disregard for halachic consequence. However, the term *anti-government* is a loaded one, implying absolute disloyalty, and it is worth defusing.

Books, Books Everywhere but Not a Real One in Sight

There is a sad story about a *ba'al teshuvah* whose father started an organization for parents against *ba'alei teshuvah*. This unfortunate soul likes to make use of the classic canard "I go into my son's home, and he doesn't have any books."

Now this is patently ridiculous. No group of people in the world has as many books as Orthodox Jews. Even the most uneducated laborer has a set of Talmud, *Chumashim*, and countless other staples of Jewish Torah literature, usually prominently displayed in the living room. This particular fellow had *sefarim* lining his walls from floor to ceiling. He had many more books than his "intelligentsia" father.

What his father meant, of course, was that there were no secular books — no books on science, history, or pop fiction; in other words, no important books. If the house had contained only a library of Oriental wisdom, exploring Tao and Confucius, or the dusty philosophies of Descartes and Nietzsche, the lack of popular books would have surely been excusable, even something to be proud of.

Hundreds of well-worn books on the wisdom of the Torah don't count.

Something to Wine About

As soon as Stanley raised his hand, I knew it would be a good one. Stanley has that rare gift of never sticking to the subject but somehow always being interesting.

"So, Rabbi, last Friday night I ate at someone's house, and after the husband made Kiddush, he started pouring the wine into these little glasses for all the guests. He had just drunk from the Kiddush cup. Isn't it kind of gross to drink from the wine he had just drunk from?"

This from a kid who'd lived in a frat house on a college campus for the past four years. Who knows what he ingested and what he'd eaten and touched? But he was bothered by a few potential germs.

"Stanley, can I ask you a question?"

"Yup."

"If I paid you ten bucks, would you drink the Kiddush wine? Is it really that repulsive to you, or are you just looking for an ax to grind?"

Sheepish grin. "Rabbi, for ten bucks I'd do just about anything."

"Right. That's what I thought. So to honor Shabbos you can drink the wine."

(Personally I pour off some wine before I drink from the cup, and especially when we have guests. Why give someone a reason to carp? — E. M.)

A Time to Defend...and a Time to Counterattack

Sometimes the best way to deal with an issue is not to address it in all its particulars. The reason for this is simple.

If you begin debating a lot of nitty-gritty technicalities, you can easily lose the attention of the audience. Often they've never really thought about the subject and are only parroting something they've read or heard somewhere else, and if you get into it too deeply, you'll lose them. So while it's worth covering the substance of the issue, try to avoid getting mired in all the little details. If anyone would like to discuss it further, that can always be done after the class.

On occasion you will feel that the audience is testing you, baiting you, just to see if you will fold under pressure. In such cases, the best approach is to fire back at the inquisitor and quickly expose the ludicrousness, and often the hypocrisy, of his position. Otherwise, you may find yourself fending off unmerited questions for the whole lesson.

This occurred at a lecture I was giving to a group of teenagers from a nonreligious kibbutz. The *madrich*, whom I had met on another occasion, had a very cynical attitude toward Judaism. He was actually a bright fellow, and I fully expect to see him in the yeshivah within the next few years. But not just yet; in the meantime, he still thinks he's got a valid worldview.

During the question-and-answer session that followed the class, this kibbutz lad said in a scornful voice, "It's nice that all these people are learning in yeshivah, but who exactly is funding them?" He was alluding to the fact that the Israeli government provides a small subsidy for yeshivah students.

I could have gotten into an ideological discussion with him about the value of Torah study to the Jewish people, especially to the secular Jews, but the forum wasn't right, and I primarily wanted to expose the duplicity of his criticism. So I replied, "You're from a kibbutz, aren't you?"

"Yeah."

"The kibbutz movement is a losing proposition financially, correct? The Israeli government, to whom I pay taxes, has been funding the kibbutzim to the tune of hundreds of millions of shekels per year. Do you have any objection to that?"

All he could offer in response was a muttered, "Well, you know, I am against that, too." But the point was made.

Party Hearty!

It's always worth remembering that if your counterattack can be made in a humorous manner, you will find that what seemed to be a hostile group has been quickly won over.

At a lecture to an anti-religious youth group, one girl asked in a belligerent tone, "What are you men doing all day while the women are out working and supporting a family?"

All eyes focused on me. I looked at her quizzically and said, "What do you think we're doing? We're at home partying and drinking beer."

The place exploded with laughter, and from that point on they were mine.

Dealing with the Primitive

It is very important to show, when addressing difficult topics, that you are not intimidated by the questions and are perfectly willing to discuss them as long as the audience is respectful. If they get out of hand, you are wasting your time and theirs.

At a lecture to a mixed audience, I discussed the beauty and the depth of Torah. Suddenly I heard from the back, "What a bunch of baloney!"

It wasn't really phrased that elegantly, but the FCC — and decency — doesn't permit me to print the real declaration.

I said, "Excuse me?" while looking around for the prodigy behind that assertion.

It turned out to be a rather bored-looking teenager draped over a chair in the back of the room, quite pleased with having imparted such a nugget of insight. Even when I made eye contact, he didn't get embarrassed at his slip; he merely repeated his remark for mine and his buddies' further edification.

Obviously, dissecting the finer points of his convictions would not work in this case, and I didn't want to cede control of the discussion to such a lout, so I simply proceeded to display his stupidity in front of everyone. Without mercy, I exposed his complete ignorance of the subject at hand.

To have let him off the hook without responding would have confirmed the audience's characterization of religious rabbis as Aramaic-spouting, spineless wimps who back down as soon as challenged. A swift rejoinder to an uncalled-for attack shows that we are "with it" and normal, often a more valuable message than the lecture itself.

For other hecklers, I have another trick I learned from an experienced pro that almost always works. If a questioner gets rowdy and won't let me finish a thought, constantly interrupting, I simply close my mouth and sit down, thus focusing the audience's attention on the heckler, and allow him to continue making a fool out of himself. Usually, after a few seconds, he will feel sufficiently ridiculous that he will slink back into his chair and keep his mouth shut for the rest of the lecture. If he doesn't catch on, the audience will often start shushing him and tell him to sit down.

Even if the heckler has got an extra-high chutzpah quotient and insists on finishing his filibuster, the following method will almost always work.

What you do is politely let him finish his thought, such as it is, and then, when he is done speaking, repeat his objections to the audience. This he will let you do, since you're quoting his own pearls of wisdom.

Then ask him, "Is that right? Is that your point?"

When he agrees that you have captured the essence of his position, proceed to demolish his argument point by point, taking no prisoners.

You will have the sympathy of the audience, who will have been dismayed at his rudeness, and even he will be unable to interrupt you, since you let him speak without interruption.

These examples may seem extreme, and, indeed, in most cases audiences are polite and considerate, but on the rare occasions that call for such measures, they are worth their weight in gold.

The Great Debate

Occasionally one gets support from the unlikeliest places. I had been invited to speak at an Arachim seminar. These are intensive, intellectual seminars directed toward high-achievement Jews, for the most part nonreligious. At the seminars, they are exposed to the Torah perspective, many for the first time in their lives. The goal is to get the attendees to begin thinking about their Judaism and to get them interested in some sort of follow-up to these seminars.

The group to whom I was speaking was a rather mixed bag, a smattering of yarmulkes sprinkled among a primarily secular audience. The common denominator was that they were all intelligent — and combative. Most of the talk consisted of a heated debate on the benefits of learning Torah versus its downsides, such as being an unproductive waste of time, a drag on society, and so forth. Opinions were flying fast and furious, and if you didn't shout a little, you didn't get heard. Not surprisingly, I was in favor of Torah learning and in a distinct minority. I'd been there before, but this group, while respectful, was proving to be a handful. They were especially scornful of men in *kollel*, who learned Torah full-time after marriage.

Suddenly I heard someone shouting from the back of the room, "I want to talk. I've got something to say!"

I looked up. A tall, distinguished-looking gentleman stood there, waving his arms for attention. He was wearing a knitted yarmulke and modern dress.

I remember thinking to myself, *Oh no, I don't need this now — a religious person who is going to come out against kollel and in support of all these secular opinions.*

I tried to avoid calling on him, but he wasn't having it. He shouted, "I haven't said anything all night. I'd like a turn to speak. I've got something to say."

With no choice, I turned the floor over to him.

He looked around the room for a few seconds and then said, "I've got three sons. The oldest is a doctor, and I'm very proud of him. He's hardworking and dedicated, and he supports himself with no handouts from anyone. My second boy is an engineer, and I'm proud of him, too. He went to college, studied hard, and made a mensch of himself."

I was cringing inside, thinking, *Uh-oh, here it comes*.

"My third son didn't want to go to college or learn a trade. He just wanted to sit in *kollel* and live like a pauper."

The audience was listening raptly and sympathetically.

The man paused for a moment. "I must tell you, I have more joy and more *nachas* from my youngest boy than from my other two sons combined. In fact, I have more pleasure from him than from anything else in my life."

The collective gasp was audible; no one expected that.

"My youngest has a beautiful family. All of his kids are a joy, so well behaved and undemanding. He may not have much money, but he has such a full and fulfilling life. If only I had known this before, I would have pushed all of my kids to learn in *kollel*."

I, for one, had nothing to add. This man had said it all for me.

I offered to sit down and allow him to finish the lecture. Everyone had a good chuckle and, more importantly, left with the correct message.

Hello, Dolly!

Tom hit me with this one in *shiur* one day.

"Rabbi, aren't you supposed to greet every person you meet?"

Sensing the next question, I reluctantly replied in the affirmative.

"Y'know, when I walk down Meah Shearim Street, I say hello to the people, and most of the religious Jews there don't reply."

I said to him, "Tom, have you gotten a good look at yourself in the mirror recently? You've got an earring, your hair looks like it's been electrocuted, you're not dressed like any human being these people have ever seen. Would you say hello to yourself on the street?"

We all had a good laugh, and then I elaborated.

"First of all, Tom, you're right. Theoretically people should greet someone who says hello to them. Sometimes, though, it's so extraordinary to be greeted by a total stranger that you're more shocked than anything else.

"Second of all, Tom, when you say people, do you mean female people, by any chance?"

Again a hearty chuckle of assent.

"Well, I'm sorry, Tom, but the female people in Meah Shearim are not going to say hello to you, no matter what you do."

Tom had never complained that no one in Manhattan ever says hello to a stranger. This complaint was reserved for Orthodox Jews.

A Burning Question

Bill Buchler raised his hand in class. "Rabbi, is it true that a Jew is not allowed to do anything that harms his health?"

Uh-oh, here it comes. The cigarette question.

"Yes, Bill, it's true. You may not intentionally harm your health."

"Then how come so many Orthodox Jews smoke?"

"Bill, are you bothered by the fact that Orthodox Jews smoke, or do you want to know what the halachic view is on smoking?"

"Yeah, yeah, whatever, gimme the halachic view."

Smoking is a delicate issue, primarily because there is almost no doubt that it is unhealthy, and there is even less doubt about the difficulty of quitting the habit. This makes it prime material for bashing the ultra-Orthodox.

What I try to do first is distinguish between what the halachah says about the subject and what Jewish people sometimes do. In other words, the fact that a religious Jew smokes doesn't mean the Torah necessarily approves of smoking. But the fact that the halachah discourages smoking also doesn't mean that the 5 percent of Orthodox Jews who do smoke are all hypocrites.

The reason for this is that it is actually a complex question as to whether smoking is forbidden or merely discouraged by halachah. There is also a distinction made between someone who is already addicted to smoking (having started before becoming aware of the halachic problems) and someone who wishes to take up smoking.

Finally, there is a difference between smoking in the privacy of one's home as opposed to smoking in public.

So a question like Bill's is a sort of catch-22, because no matter what I say about smoking, Bill is going to jump on me.

Of course, the guy who asks this question is usually an avid bungee-jumper, parasailer, and recreational big-wave surfer who thinks nothing of driving well above the speed limit. But he's concerned about the dangers of smoking.

A Matter of Respect

"Rabbi, do we respect other religions?"

The answer to this is similar to the one that was given to Sid Fishman.

"What do you mean by respect? Does respect mean we attach credibility to their beliefs? Then no, not at all. We don't believe that what the Christians say is true. It is actually impossible for us to agree with their theology, because part of their theology is that Judaism is wrong. Obviously we can't both be right.

"Thus, the two religions are mutually exclusive from the standpoint of absolute truth. But it doesn't mean that we curse out the religion and its practices either. We simply don't agree with their beliefs.

"And if you are referring to respecting the individual, as a person and as a creation of God, then the answer is absolutely. We are beholden to respect each and every person, regardless of his or her religious affiliation.

"Every human being has an element of Godliness in him, and as such deserves respect. The Talmud specifically enjoins us to give honor to an elderly gentile. So, like most things, it really depends on how you define respect."

TV or Not TV

Here's a question we've all run into at one time or another, and it is worth having a clear understanding of how to deal with it.

"Rabbi, are you against television?"

"Absolutely not. I'm only against the programming."

"But do you have a TV in your house, Rabbi?"

"Nope."

"Are you serious?" This in an incredulous tone of voice, as if I had just suggested reintroducing human sacrifice.

"Absolutely."

"But don't you think you are depriving your children? I mean, they'll grow up unaware."

"Unaware of what?"

A pause. "Well, you know, unaware of what's going on in the world. They're so sheltered. How will they know what's going on out there? It's all very nice if they remain in the cloistered (another favorite word) world of the yeshivah, but what if they want to go into business or a profession?"

"Can I ask you a question? And I'm asking this to the entire group. Can any of you name the premier of China?"

That question is invariably followed by silence, a few brave guesses, and a lot of head-scratching, but never once has anyone been able to answer it correctly.

Now it's my turn to be incredulous. "Do you mean that not one of you can tell me the name of the premier of China? The head of the largest country in the world, with a population of 1.2 billion people, and none of you know his name. What are you, sheltered?"

Embarrassed silence.

Everyone focuses on what is important to him in life. Once you get past the essentials, reading, writing, arithmetic — and always look both ways before crossing the street — every person must choose which nonessentials are important to him. It is impossible to possess all knowledge, so we must be selective.

Everyone concentrates on studying and knowing that which he believes is worthwhile. He will try to block out anything that will hamper that development, either consciously or subconsciously.

Clearly the premier of China and the Indonesian system of government are not important to the boys, while the latest *Hard Copy* and *Seinfeld* are. That's why they know all about Jerry, but they don't know who the premier of China is.

"Well, Torah Jews also don't spend much spare time on Jiang Zemin or on the parliament of India, but instead of focusing on the Power Rangers, we teach our kids Torah.

"That's because we consider Torah to be the most worthwhile 'nonessential' in the world — in fact, the only worthwhile 'nonessential.'

"Most nine-year-old cheder boys know a large chunk of the Mishnah, almost all 613 mitzvos, and tens of Torah-themed books, but they don't know Chinese culture. Their secular counterparts know movies and rap, and they also don't know Chinese culture.

"As far as not surviving in the world without television, that is patently ridiculous. We have lawyers, doctors, and businessmen galore. To the best of my knowledge, Albert Einstein grew up without a television, as did Jonas Salk.

"The great success stories of today's business world are not the kids who vegetated in front of the TV as youngsters, but the geeky, studious types, such as Bill Gates, Jerry Yang, and the rest of Silicon Valley."

Actually, recently one young member of the audience did know the correct answer to my question. He was a *frum* FFB who had never owned a TV.

A Stone's Throw

"Hey, Rabbi, why do *frum* Jews throw stones at cars on Shabbos?"

"Um, to get exercise?"

"No, no, seriously, why do they do it?"

"Well, who told you that they do?"

"Come on, everyone talks about it, and even the *Jerusalem Post* mentions it. So don't try to dodge the issue. Everyone knows they throw stones."

"Okay, Josh, here's the story. Number one, anyone who does throw stones is wrong for doing so. There is no excuse. However, I'm not convinced it's really that rampant. I've lived in Jerusalem for years and have never seen anyone throw a stone at a car or a person. Not once!"

"You do realize that even handling stones is forbidden on Shabbos. So it's doubtful that all the *frum* Jews are violating the Sabbath in order to prevent its violation by secular people.

"But for the sake of *shalom*, I'll grant you that an occasional inorganic geologic spherule does get tossed at an occasional automobile and that the tosser is otherwise religious. No one ever claimed that Torah society is perfect. On the contrary, the Torah was given to us in order to perfect us. We've also got some unruly elements in our midst. The people throwing stones are, for the most part, bored teenagers, not mature adults."

"Yeah, maybe, but where are the parents? Why aren't they watching their kids?"

"Josh, when you were a teenager, did your parents have one hundred percent control over you? Did they even have fifty percent control over you?"

Josh laughs. "Uh, no! I don't think so."

"So you can't really expect these parents to have complete control over their teenagers."

"I still think the Torah should teach them not to do this."

"They are taught not to do it, but I want you to know a very important truth. If you ever see flaws in people who are totally observant and are identified with the Torah community, I want you to remember: you are seeing a flaw in the person, not in the Torah. The Torah they are learning is still perfect. Torah teaches goodness and improves anyone who studies it. But it doesn't always work immediately.

"All you need to do is look at the general crime statistics for observant Jews to be convinced of this. The crime rate is practically nonexistent. I know non-Jews who live in religious Jewish neighborhoods, where they are totally out of place and don't have much social interaction, because they know it is crime-free and safe.

"So if you see a person who has studied Torah, and he is not acting as he should be, I can only tell you one thing: Just imagine how this same person would be acting without having studied Torah!"

Uncovered!

"Rabbi, can I talk to you?"

"Sure, Jeff, what's on your mind?"

"I was at a lecture the other day, and they were talking about King David and Bathsheba. The rabbi giving the lecture said that the Talmud says King David did not sin with Bathsheba."

"Yes, that's true. That is what the Gemara says."

"Well, Rabbi, quite frankly, it looks to me like a coverup. I mean, let's be real. If David did that and sent her husband away and all that, then he must have sinned. He was human. I thought this is a religion in which we are intellectually honest. Why the coverup?"

"Jeff, let me explain something to you. Are you familiar with the Bible?"

"A little."

"Have you ever heard of Abraham?"

"Oh, yeah, sure."

"Adam? Noah?"

"Definitely."

"I want you to look at the Torah and pick out any name you recognize."

"Okay, how about Moses."

"Very good. Now pick another name."

"Aaron."

"You just picked the names of two very prominent people in the Torah. Do you know that both of them are criticized in the Torah, and rather severely? On their level, they stepped out of line, and the Torah takes them to task on that. Are you aware of that?"

"No, I never knew that."

"Oh yes. Moses is criticized for getting angry and then hitting the rock, and Aaron is criticized for helping to create the golden calf, despite his worthy intentions. These would have been minor sins for people like us, but for people of their great stature, they were considered failings, and the Torah doesn't duck the issue. It lambasts them.

"Did you know that Abraham is criticized for doubting God? And Jacob is questioned for having married two sisters? Do you know that Joseph was criticized for bringing a negative report about his brothers?

"Just about every single great person that you can find in the Torah has a criticism aimed at something they have done. So when you accuse the Rabbis of covering up for David and Bathsheba, I must correct you.

"This is a religious system in which we don't cover anything up. If there is a criticism, we mention it. We are meant to learn positive lessons from the shortcomings and imperfections of our forebears. We don't pretend that humans are born perfect; rather, we strive to become perfect. So if anything negative comes up, we are honest about it. We don't cover it up.

"When the Sages in the Talmud, whose every word is based on long tradition, tell me that there was no sin, I believe it. I know they're not covering up for our heroes and our leaders.

"When they say there was no *aveirah*, it means that the whole story of King David and Bathsheba was not a tawdry sin, but was something much deeper than meets the eye. There is a moral lesson to be learned from the story. But it is certainly not a coverup."

Men's Lib

"Rabbi, don't you think Judaism is chauvinistic?"
"Toward the men or toward the women?"
"Really, Rabbi, seriously!"
"Oh, seriously? In that case, no, I don't think so."

I've been asked this question many times, by both women and men from all walks of life. The one common denominator is that, almost exclusively, the questioner is not an Orthodox woman. For some reason, they themselves almost never feel discriminated against. I guess they're just so beaten down that they can't even summon up the will to question it. But...seriously.

When this issue is brought up, a discussion usually ensues showing how Judaism really does respect women and how most Orthodox women feel fulfilled and content with their role in life, certainly to a greater degree than your average nonreligious woman. There is plenty of empirical data to draw upon and even more anecdotal and logical evidence supporting these conclusions. In addition, we usually touch on the main highlights of feminism versus Torah Judaism.

So when Tom asked me the following question, I was not at all put off.

"But, Rabbi, don't you think you are a little harsh on the women?"

"No, Tom. Try to remember the way you treated women during your four years in university. I'll bet that was pretty harsh. How much respect did you show for women?

"Unlike most of the world's social systems, Torah Judaism never treats women as objects. Have you ever heard a feminist complain that in the Torah system the man has a halachic obligation, when he gets married, to support his family? A woman has no such obligation. Why don't the feminists ever complain about that? If the system was truly a man-made system, invented by the 'chauvinistic' rabbis, then why didn't the men obligate the women to support the family? That way the men could sit in a hammock all day and drink premium lager."

In fact, there is no system in the world in which women are so respected, and as equal to men, as in Orthodox Judaism. The respective roles of men and women may be very different, but the relative importance of those roles is indistinguishable. In ethical, moral, and legal matters, this equality and appreciation is amply demonstrated and remarked upon, going all the way back to the original male-female relationship in the Torah, that of Adam and Chavah.

The Torah describes Chavah as "*ezer kenegdo* — a helpmeet next to him." The woman is a partner who works in the same line, but at a different point on that line. Neither is above or below the other; they are merely different. It is obvious that if God intended man and woman to be exactly the same, he would have just created another man; there would be no need to fashion a woman. And if they're exactly the same, why would the Torah proclaim that "it is no good for man to be alone; I will create for him a helpmeet," implying that the creation of this helpmeet will make the world "good." How can two identical no-good creatures change the world from no good to good? Obviously, the woman was not just a duplication of man, but a new element, which, in unison with man, could bring perfection and goodness to the world.

These sources are not secret. The information is available to anyone who wishes to discover it. Of course, if a person examines Torah with a preconceived agenda, he can certainly find apparent inequalities, as with anything examined with preconceptions.

One day I was in a playful mood. We had been talking about the realities of marriage, role differentiation, and other women's issues. The audience was pretty cynical, and I felt a change of pace was needed.

I picked up my keys and jingled them.

A guy said to me, "Why are you jingling your keys?"

"I have to go home and unlock my wife. She's chained to the wall right now. I only let her out when I get home."

The point was well taken.

O Higher State

I spent a beautiful Shabbos once at Ohio State University as a guest of the local Hillel House. We had a very nice davening followed by a beautiful Shabbos meal, with lots of singing, and some words of Torah. About thirty-five Jewish students came to the meal, which ended at about eleven.

Exhausted from a long week, I was anxious to get some sleep. I started heading up to my room, when the Hillel director saw me and said, "Hold on a second. The night is yet young. I want to show you how the other half lives."

He took me out for a walk around the area. The name of the avenue was High Street, appropriately enough, and the director showed me the sights.

Never having lived on a college campus, I was amazed to see the long lines of people shouting and carrying on in their efforts to get into the bars and discos all along the street. The police turned up and put up a blockade along the sidewalk to stop the overflow of people from spilling out into the traffic.

All I could think was "*Ashreinu mah tov chelkeinu — Praiseworthy is our lot!*" as I compared this wild scene to the tranquil Shabbos meal from which I had just come.

Now I tell people that I went to Ohio State University and got a real education.

Halachic Issues

HALACHIC ISSUES

People who get involved in *kiruv* often face situations where they feel that they must compromise their standards of *Yiddishkeit* in order to succeed in their mission. Obviously doing something that is against the halachah is unacceptable, no matter what the end goal is. It is ridiculous for a person to violate the halachah in order that another person should keep the halachah.

However, sometimes the matter under consideration does not involve a clear violation of halachah, but more of a gray area, or even just a question of *lechatchilah* versus *bedieved*, where if one would search, one may find a *heter*, a leniency.

I cannot attempt to deal with all such situations here or even to tell anyone what general attitude to adopt. I simply want to share with you one story in which a person chose not to rely on a leniency, resulting in a greater *kiddush Hashem*.

The story was told to my father by Rabbi Gavriel Ginsburg, the *rosh yeshivah* of Ner Israel in Toronto. It happened to an Orthodox young man of Rabbi Ginsburg's acquaintance.

This fellow was on a business trip with a very tight schedule, and he had not had a chance to eat anything all day. Finally he boarded a night flight for Toronto and gratefully sank into the comfortable aisle seat he had been prudent enough to reserve in advance. Now if only the airline would come through with his specially ordered kosher meal, he would feel like a mensch again.

After takeoff, the flight attendants started serving the evening meal, and they handed our friend a special kosher meal. He thanked the stewardess, then realized that he would have to wait another few minutes before he could get up to wash on the bread. He couldn't leave his seat yet, since the crew was still serving the other passengers.

In the meantime, he opened the double-wrapped sandwich and peeked at the contents. A delicious-looking pastrami sandwich peered right back at him.

Finally the aisles cleared, the seatbelt sign switched off, and our hungry protagonist rose to wash. He washed his hands, made a *berachah*, and started back down the aisle. As he walked, he was suddenly struck by a terrible thought. He had left the unwrapped sandwich sitting on his tray for several minutes, with no one guarding it. Jewish law mandates that all kosher meat must be under Jewish supervision from the time of slaughter until it is eaten to make sure it has not been switched with less expensive non-kosher meat. A double seal is also acceptable, but our starving hero had opened the seal on his sandwich.

During the short trip back to his seat, his mind whirled as he tried to find some way he could possibly partake of the meal. He considered the idea that this law referred to a commercial situation, where there was a profit motive, but not to a private meal, where there was no reason for anyone to switch the meat in his sandwich.

Besides, he had been away from his seat for only three minutes. Why on earth would anyone steal his sandwich when he could just ask the stewardess for another one? And what kind of whacko would trade sandwiches with him? Even if someone was really hungry, he would just eat his own, not trade with him. In any case, it was only a rabbinical enactment, not a biblical rule.

To make a long story short, by the time he reached his seat, he had almost convinced himself that the law didn't apply in this case and he could eat his sandwich.

He sat down, and there was his sandwich, sitting in its kosher wrapper just as he had left it. Just to make doubly sure, however, he again peeked inside the sandwich, and sure enough, it was the same pastrami he had left there.

He made a *berachah*, ate a corner of the bread, and suddenly decided, *No! I am not eating this sandwich. I don't care if it is the same sandwich. I'm not eating it. The Rabbis made a rule, and even if it's not really relevant in this case, I'm going to stick to it.* Resolutely he pushed the meal away and, ignoring the hunger pangs in his stomach, took out a *sefer* and started learning.

The fellow seated next to him looked at him queerly and said, "Excuse me, sir, but aren't you going to eat that sandwich?"

He looked up. "No, I'm not really hungry."

"You aren't? You sure looked hungry before. And isn't that why you washed your hands? So you could eat? What made you change your mind so suddenly?"

Our friend didn't feel like explaining the whole story to this fellow, especially since it wouldn't make much sense. Also, maybe the guy would get insulted at being suspected of thievery. So he just laughed it off and said, "Yes, I don't really know why. I just don't feel like eating now."

But his neighbor wouldn't be brushed off so easily, and he persisted in his questioning.

Finally the Jew couldn't avoid the truth any longer, and he told his seatmate the reason he wasn't eating. He was a little embarrassed, so he finished by saying, "Look, I know it probably sounds crazy to you, but that's our custom, so I've got to follow it."

The gentile regarded him strangely and then leaned over and said, "Sir, your God must be watching over you. I've always wondered what kosher meat tastes like, so when you went to wash, I switched pastrami sandwiches with you, thinking you'd never notice."

Halachah is the set of rules that guide us through life, and these rules are meant to be followed even when we don't completely understand their validity in a particular situation. However, sometimes we merit, in a flash of insight, to see the brilliant underpinnings of this incredible system.

— E. M.

A Valid Question

A young man whose name I didn't even know stopped me in the hall one day.

"Are you Rabbi Kaplan?"

"Yes."

"I heard you're a *kohen*."

"Yes. One of many."

"Okay, good. Can I ask you a question about *kohanim*?"

"Sure, no problem."

I was expecting an easy question, like whether a *kohen* gets to pick the best bed in the dorm room.

"Okay, this is the story. My dad is a *kohen* and he's married to my mom, but it's her second marriage. The first ended in divorce. Doesn't that mean I'm somehow stigmatized?"

Not quite what I was expecting at eleven o'clock in the morning while heading from one *shiur* to another.

Normally I'd have asked him to come to the office to speak with him privately and get his whole background. But he seemed to know already that there was a problem and merely wanted confirmation.

I answered, "Look, I'm not a halachic authority. For a final decision you'd have to speak to one, but this much I'll say. If it is as you say, and your mom was legitimately married according to halachah and then halachically divorced, then yes, there is some stigma. You would be considered a *challal*, a blemished *kohen*. You can marry into the Jewish people, but you wouldn't have all the bylaws of a regular *kohen*. But again, please speak to a qualified halachic authority."

"That's what I thought. Thanks a lot!"

Just like that. Whatever happened to the questions about forgetting *Ya'aleh V'Yavo* during *bentch*ing?

The Once-in-a-Lifetime Visit

There was one student who, while in Israel, went to visit the grave of his grandfather for the very first time. While in the cemetery, he was apprised of a rather startling piece of information. He was a *kohen*.

He realized this when he saw a pair of hands engraved on the tombstone in the manner of the *birkas kohanim*, the priestly blessing. That cut the visit short.

What Fee? It's an Honorarium!

Everyone knows about the Jewish law of circumcision, the removal of the foreskin, which is performed on a baby boy after eight days and brings him into the Jewish fold as a full-fledged member of the Jewish people. What is not as widely known, or as commonly performed, is the mitzvah of *pidyon haben*, literally, "redemption of the firstborn son."

Essentially the idea is that the firstborn child is consecrated unto the service of God and must be redeemed by his parents from the priestly community in order to be freed of his obligation of Temple service. The reason it is less frequently performed is because this commandment is relevant only if one's firstborn child was born by natural childbirth and the father or mother is not a *kohen* or a Levi.

The *pidyon haben* is performed on the thirtieth day of the child's life and is usually celebrated with a festive meal, along with little packets of sugar and garlic that are distributed to all the guests.

The actual ritual consists of the parents giving the *kohen* five silver coins in exchange for their son. Since today most people do not own silver coins, the custom is to buy these special coins from the *kohen* for their real value and then to perform the ritual using the just-bought coins, leaving the *kohen* with a small profit.

It is perfectly all right for the *kohen* to accept this gift, since this is one of the ways in which the Torah provided for the priests' livelihood, thus allowing them to spend their days teaching and serving the people. My wife, however, always feels guilty about my taking the money. She looks at it as though I were profiting from my religious status.

In my case, being a relatively young *kohen* on the staff of a rather large *ba'al teshuvah* yeshivah, I get plenty of business. This is because many of the students are firstborn sons and were not redeemed as babies by their parents. They are therefore required to redeem themselves in their adult years. Often the first they have ever heard of this unique mitzvah is upon their arrival in yeshivah.

At first I didn't have my own silver coins to use for the mitzvah, and I would borrow them from another *kohen*. But soon, due to the volume of business, I decided to invest in my own silver coins. They cost me 110 Israeli shekels, then worth about thirty dollars.

Soon after I had bought the silver coins, three different guys in Ohr Somayach learned about their *pidyon* obligation, and each asked me if I would perform the *pidyon haben* ceremony for them. Always happy to oblige, I agreed. When I told my wife about the triple-header, she again told me that she felt funny about my getting paid for doing a mitzvah. I told her that the whole idea is for the *kohen* to receive a gift for his spiritual services, but she wasn't buying it.

When the respective *pidyon*-ees asked me what I charged for my services, I gave them what has since become my standard answer: "The set fee is seventy shekels, but you can give what you feel it is worth to you."

Well, what do you know, the first guy gave me fifty shekels, the second gave me forty shekels, and the last fellow thought it was worth only twenty. The total: one hundred and ten shekels, exactly what I had just paid for my new coins.

I couldn't ask for a clearer sign from Heaven, or at least that's what I told my wife.

When another student, Wallace, a newly religious young man whose parents had never redeemed him, asked me about my fee, I gave him my standard reply about paying what it was worth to him. He reached into his wallet and pulled out three hundred-dollar bills. That's a lot of money for five minutes' work. Priestly gift or not, I couldn't take it. I thanked Wallace kindly and took a single bill.

I have since learned that when a clergyman takes money for something, it's not called a fee; it's called an honorarium. I'm going to have to explain that to my wife. Maybe that will make her feel better.

My Name Is Rabbi Kaplan; I Am with the KGB

Then there was the Russian couple who had been persuaded by an observant friend to arrange a bris milah for their newborn son. When the baby turned one month old, the rabbi who had taken care of the circumcision called me to request that I perform the *pidyon haben* for the child. I gladly agreed and felt fortunate that I could help a young immigrant couple perform this mitzvah.

On the appointed day, I set off to perform my priestly duties. I found the small apartment with some difficulty, knocked on the door, and was greeted warmly by the proud new father. I looked around, expecting to find a happy, beaming mother, and found her cowering in a corner, clearly nervous and worried.

I'm not such a scary-looking person, so I couldn't fathom what she was worried about. I greeted her with a reassuring smile, and I decided to set her mind at ease by giving her baby a kiss. Not seeing the baby in the room, I said to the mother, "Where is the baby?"

She looked at me suspiciously and said, "Why? What are you going to do to him?"

It suddenly dawned on me what the poor woman was so nervous about. The last time a bushy-bearded rabbi had invaded their little home, he'd taken a knife to her little baby. She had only recently arrived from Russia, and that was probably the first bris she had ever seen. The poor woman was terrified, and there was no way she was going to let anything like that happen again.

I quickly explained to her that this was a totally painless procedure, and the baby would not be harmed, exchanged, improved upon, or altered. It was simply a symbolic transaction between her husband and myself. That calmed her a little, but she still kept a suspicious eye on me until I had safely returned her baby.

After the ceremony, the couple graciously invited me to join them for the festive celebratory meal. They assured me that everything had the proper *hechsher*, and it would be no problem for me to participate in the meal.

Before accepting, I sneaked into the living room and took a quick glance at the comestibles beautifully spread out on the table. The cold cuts looked delicious and were indeed kosher.

So was the cream cheese that had been spread on the cold cuts.

I politely declined the invitation.

A Restful Grave

On a class trip up north, a group of yeshivah students went to visit the holy Ari's grave, located in Tzefas. Since the grave is poorly marked, the *kohanim* were required to wait outside for the rest of the group. They sat down on one of those ubiquitous Israeli concrete benches to rest, until they realized that it wasn't a concrete bench — it was a concrete tombstone.

If You Say So

Then there are the well-meaning bystanders who are always happy to render a halachic decision for you.

Once I went to visit a close family member in the hospital, but when I arrived, I could not determine whether or not it was halachically permissible for me, a *kohen*, to enter.

Some hospitals in Israel post signs letting the *kohanim* know if anyone has passed away in the hospital recently and the body has not yet been removed from the building, in which case the *kohen* would be forbidden from entering the hospital.

Since there was no sign at this hospital, I wasn't sure what to do, so I remained outside until I could find someone who might help me.

The security guard, a secular Jew, saw me pacing back and forth. He approached me and asked, "What are you doing here?"

"Well, I'm a *kohen*, and I'm not sure if I'm allowed in the hospital."

"Oh, don't worry about it. *Kohanim* are allowed!"

"Really, how do you know?"

"Oh, I'm a *kohen*, and I enter all the time."

A Reliable Halachic Authority?

That reminds me of the time I got stuck in Manhattan for Shabbos. I was on a bus with two other teenagers, and we sat in traffic for five hours on the Palisades.

When we finally got to Manhattan, there were exactly twelve minutes left until Shabbos, and we had nowhere to go. Thankfully one of us had a credit card, and we dashed into the nearest hotel, throwing our wallets on the floor as we ran in. I rushed up to the front desk and practically yelled at the guy standing there, "Quick! Gimme a room. I need a room before Shabbos."

The fellow looked at me calmly and said, "Relax, young man. I used to be a Reform rabbi, and you've still got time. As you know, there are two *shki'ot*, biblical and rabbinical. Now is only the rabbinical sunset."

Just what I needed — a former Reform rabbi telling me how to keep Shabbos.

— E. M.

Mixed-Up Minhagim

The following story was told by a certain rabbi in South America. One evening a woman called his home, asking for the rabbi. The rabbi took the phone. "Hello."

"Rabbi, I have a question for you."

"Yes, ma'am."

"We have a *minhag* in my family to eat strictly kosher the entire month of Elul."

"Okay, so what's the question?"

"Well, like I said, we have this *minhag*, but we're not quite sure if it begins on the first day of Rosh Chodesh or the second day."

Mitzvah Movie

On the subject of *minhagim*, one of my students told me that his family had a *minhag* to attend a movie every Thanksgiving eve. He wanted to know if he should go.

I told him, "Absolutely not!"

He agreed, but he just wanted to know if he needed to be *matir neder* (absolve himself of a binding commitment).

I told him he should call Steven Spielberg.

Be Gentile, Doctor

A friend of mine is a rabbi in a large metropolitan city, but one with a rather limited Jewish population. As a result, those Jews who do come to speak with the rabbi are often somewhat interesting, to put it mildly.

One day a woman came to see him with a seemingly straightforward request. She was expecting a baby boy, and her husband, a doctor, wanted to perform the circumcision. He was willing to get instruction from a traditional *mohel*, and even to have the *mohel* present during the procedure.

Now this woman was quite religious; in fact, she told the rabbi that she had requested that the hospital assign her room 613 when she gave birth, since that is the amount of the mitzvos in the Torah.

Additionally, she had postponed her wedding date when she

learned that it conflicted with a traditional Jewish mourning period. She did not want to have a personal celebration in the midst of communal mourning. So we were talking about a fine, upstanding Jewish woman. Not only that, but her husband was a children's doctor, so from a medical standpoint he was even somewhat qualified for the job.

The rabbi explained that her husband would have to undergo some training and have a certified *mohel* attend at the circumcision, but that otherwise it was perfectly okay for the father to perform the bris. In fact, it is a special mitzvah to circumcise one's own son rather than use an agent to do so.

After he had rendered his decision, however, he noticed that the woman still seemed somewhat uncomfortable, so he inquired, "What's the matter? Are you afraid to have your husband perform the bris milah?"

"Oh no, Rabbi. That's not it, not at all. He's a wonderful doctor. It's just that my husband, well, you see, Rabbi, he's a goy."

The rabbi would have burst out laughing if he hadn't felt so much like crying.

— E. M.

Charity Begins at Home

Occasionally halachah, like anything involving Judaism, can turn political.

I was giving a lecture on the laws of *tzedakah*, and a hand went up in the back. It was, typically, a former yeshivah high school student; the rest of the audience were *ba'alei teshuvah*.

"Rabbi, what is the Torah's attitude toward giving *tzedakah* to non-Jews?"

A seemingly innocent question, but a loaded one, which, taken the wrong way, can make Orthodoxy seem biased and insular.

"That is a very good question, and I'm glad you asked it.

"According to the letter of the law, we are not obligated to give *tzedakah* to non-Jews. Not because we don't like them, but because we have an obligation to take care of our own family first. If a person has a poor brother and a poor cousin, and he has only enough money to support one of them, his first obligation is to help his brother."

"But how about the rest of the world? Don't we care about them?" The standard, predictable response.

"Believe me, if the Jews would take care of the Jews, and the Christians would take care of the Christians, and the Muslims would take care of the Muslims, no one would have anything to worry about. Ronald Reagan, as president of the United States, the world's richest country, gave only eight hundred dollars to charity over an entire year. And that money went to a museum. The problem is not that Jews only take care of their fellow Jews."

"But what about nowadays? Does that mean Jews don't give charity to non-Jews nowadays?"

"Well, there is a concept called '*darkei shalom.*' *Darkei shalom* means that in order to maintain peaceful coexistence with our gentile neighbors, we may give a nominal donation if they would ask for charity, because if we wouldn't, there would be a negative backlash against the Jewish community. And, of course, we should contribute to community causes, such as policemen's and firemen's benevolent funds, since we all benefit from them and therefore have an obligation to contribute. But our first obligation is to our family. We have nothing against non-Jews. As long as they are not putting us in ovens or burning us at the stake, we are perfectly content to live and let live."

"Do you mean to say that all Jews tithe their money?"

"I don't know if all Jews tithe their money, but they should. Some Jews I know even give 20 percent of their income to charity. I can't speak for everyone, but certainly the people in my circles all tithe."

"Wow, that's unbelievable, Rabbi."

It really is. We often take our high standards for granted, forgetting that the behavior of a Torah Jew is truly unbelievable.

Vegging Out

Many *ba'alei teshuvah* are vegetarians. I'm not sure why this is so, but it could be a result of their incipient search for spirituality and meaning. In any case, I am often asked by students if there is anything wrong with being a vegetarian from a religious point of view.

I tell them that for the most part vegetarianism is not a halachic issue, except on Shabbos and *yom tov*. We are obligated to eat meat on those days in honor of the day. However, if a person genuinely dislikes meat and cannot bring himself to eat even a small piece in honor of Shabbos and *yom tov* because it is unpalatable or for health reasons, he is not obligated to do so.

That is from a purely halachic aspect. If, however, one believes that we as humans are not allowed to kill animals (and/or that animals have rights), then one is in contention with God, Who says that not only may we eat meat, but we are obligated to do so several times a year.

The same applies to protesting against cruelty in meat production. If one's problem is only with the method employed in production, then it is permissible to protest. If one believes that it is wrong to slaughter animals in general, then it becomes impermissible. In any case, just as a practical matter, protesting is probably just a waste of energy.

Once I was sitting at a Shabbos table, and a young lady, who was a vegetarian, was present.

When the customary fish was served, I asked her, "Do you only refrain from eating meat? How about fish?"

She said self-righteously, "Rabbi, if it's got a heartbeat, I don't eat it."

"Well, neither do I. I make sure it's dead first."

A Bitul Too Late

Zach Daniels has perhaps the most remarkable sense of humor I've ever come across. He's always ready with a quip or a wry observation. Zach came to yeshivah with absolutely no religious background and after becoming committed to Torah, he felt, perhaps unwisely, that he should write to his brother, who had intermarried and with whom Zach had a very warm relationship, and explain the Orthodox approach to intermarriage.

Zach penned a very sensitive, caring letter, being extremely careful not to attack his brother's lifestyle or even to suggest to him how to lead his life. He simply felt that his brother had the right to know about the heritage to which he had never been exposed.

Zach sent off his missive and waited for his brother's response in their weekly e-mail exchange, but it didn't come.

Zach sent off a lighthearted e-mail without bringing up the issue, but still no reply. He waited three months with a grudging measure of admiration for his brother's self-control, but still no reply. The message was clear: big brother was upset. Zach eventually called to make amends, and they had an amiable conversation, but there was a distance. The damage had been done.

Soon after this incident, our class was studying tractate *Gittin*, which deals with the laws of Jewish divorce.

One day the discussion turned to the concept of *bitul*, which refers to a husband's ability to nullify a bill of divorce even after he has already sent it to his wife via proxy. All the man has to do is say the word *bitul*. As long as the bill of divorce has not yet been delivered, it is nullified. Zach turned to me with a wistful look. "Rebbe, is it possible to do *bitul* on an e-mail?"

It was a joke, but one tinged with a bitter flavor.

A Batting Average of .100

Another young fellow in the yeshivah once wrote a letter home in which he detailed ten halachically based reasons why he could not stay at his parents' home for Rosh HaShanah.

His father was a Conservative Jew, but one who had studied quite a bit of halachah. He responded to his son's letter, disagreeing on every point, also from a halachic standpoint.

The student, now feeling like he was in over his head, went to speak with one of the prominent rabbis in Ohr Somayach.

The rabbi read the letters and proceeded to prove to the boy that nine of the ten reasons he had set forth were incorrect from a halachic standpoint. He had been wrong ninety percent of the time. And the one point on which he did not err wasn't reason enough to upset his family.

This was a classic case of a *ba'al teshuvah* who was worried about doing the wrong thing, which is very commendable. But instead of consulting with a more knowledgeable person and finding a halachic solution, his zeal for a mitzvah almost wound up with him transgressing one of the Ten Commandments — and alienating his family to boot.

Sorry, I Don't Rely on God

My father was once forced to spend a Shabbos in Poland, and the only place that even advertised itself as kosher was a certain camp for displaced Eastern European Jews. The spiritual leader of this camp was a graduate of the Jewish Theological Seminary, which is a Conservative school, but this man was known to be personally observant. With Shabbos approaching and no other alternative, my father made his way to this camp, expecting to be able to partake of the advertised kosher meals.

Upon arrival, however, he realized that the kashrus was not quite up to par, and so he decided not to eat anything but vegetables and bread. To my father's great surprise, he noticed that the camp rabbi was also eating nothing but vegetables.

My father said, "Look, I don't mean to be rude, but if you don't trust the kashrus, why don't you do something about it? After all, you're the rabbi here."

The rabbi answered, "Oh, I have no problem with the kashrus. It's just that when God created the world, man was not allowed to eat animals, and that is why I am not partaking of the meat."

Puzzled, my father said, "But surely you know that after the flood God permitted the consumption of animals. It says so explicitly in the Torah."

The Conservative rabbi smiled and, shaking his head almost pityingly, said, "Rabbi, if there is anyone I would expect to understand, it would be you. I don't rely on *heterim*."

— E. M.

The Philosophers

THE PHILOSOPHERS

One of the classic approaches to *kiruv* has been the lengthy discussion of deep philosophical issues, such as faith, the existence of God, and the ramifications thereof. Many *kiruv* programs also present esoteric philosophy classes, analyzing the classic philosophers through the ages.

My experience has been that while many young people have confronted the issues of faith and religion in their own lives, there are many young people who are not even aware of these questions, much less bothered by them. It may be that youngsters today are not as idealistic as young adults were in the past, are not searching on a philosophical level, and thus their commitment to Judaism is not much enhanced by understanding why we reject Spinoza, Kant, and all the others. Often it's the first they've ever heard of these arguments.

It's hard enough teaching these novice students Torah. Why confuse them with the convoluted reasoning of the Sophists only in order to prove they are false?

So That's Why They Called Him God-zilla

Among the many discussions on faith and divinity that I've had over the years, the one with Bernie stands out.

"Rabbi, are you convinced that the Sinai experience consisted of God giving the Torah to the Jewish people?"

"Yes, Bernie, I am."

"Well, how do you know it was God? Maybe it was some outer-space monster that gave the Torah."

The precise theological benefit of his reasoning escaped me, since personally I would rather be beholden to a kindly, beneficent God than to an alien monster. Bernie, however, in his reluctance to commit to Torah, seemed to feel that anything was preferable to God, even Jabba the Hutt.

The "Rabbis"

Three young fellows showed up at the yeshivah one day. They were studying at Hebrew Union College, the Reform rabbinical seminary, and they wanted to debate Jewish theology with an Orthodox rabbi.

We discussed different subjects for a while, and then I asked them the following question.

"Isn't it true that in Reform Judaism halachah is not considered binding?"

Two of them immediately answered, "No, that's not true at all."

The third guy said, "Yes, it is true. We don't believe halachah is binding."

The three of them argued about it for a while, until the third guy convinced his friends of his point of view. His reasoning was actually flawless. He said that since the Torah itself is not divine, its laws obviously can't be binding, because how could a human bind another with his man-made laws?

I didn't get involved in this discussion; I just sat back and watched in amazement.

Here we had three young men studying for the rabbinate, and they couldn't agree on the most fundamental aspect of their belief: Do they or don't they have to listen to the Torah?

It was positively frightening. This wasn't some esoteric philosophical abstraction about life after death or the meaning of life; this was the foundation of Judaism, and these future "rabbis" didn't have a clue.

Left without a Responsa

In a similar vein, I was once party to a discussion between an Orthodox *ba'alebos* and a young Reform theology student of our acquaintance regarding the obligatory nature of halachah. This layman is a sharp and clever man, but not, in any sense, a trained philosopher or an expert theologian. During the course of the conversation, the young student mentioned a Reform book of responsa, which addressed questions of Jewish law.

One of the book's queries was, is fasting on the seventeenth of Tammuz mandatory? (The seventeenth of Tammuz is a very sad day in Jewish history.) A long, detailed *teshuvah*, replete with Talmudic points of reference, was given to resolve this question.

The man listened intently to the Talmudic analysis and then said to the student, "I've got just one question for you. If halachah is not binding, how can there even be a book of responsa? Nothing is mandatory. Everyone can just do whatever they want."

The poor guy just sat there speechless. He had never thought about it. He had just swallowed the predigested mixture of Judaism, New Age, and Christianity that passes for modern-day theology and never once stopped to wonder if any of it made sense.

Nine Lives Dog Food

Greg Danielowitz came into yeshivah asking all sorts of questions about Judaism. He was a bright guy, and I enjoyed talking to him.

One day I asked him, "Greg, do you believe in an afterlife?"

"Nope."

"Well, what's gonna happen after you die?"

"Nothing. Absolutely nothing."

I'd had this conversation many times over the years and had used many different methods of refutation in addressing it. This time, for some reason, a new approach came to mind. I said to him, "Okay, Greg, so after you die, nothing will happen?"

"Right."

"Will you be aware of anything?"

"Nope."

"There'll be no continuity?"

"No."

He was so certain, so sure that he really believed what he was saying. So I asked him, "Do you mind, Greg, if after you die, we use your body for dog food?"

"Uh, nooo, no, I don't want you using my body for dog food." Quickly adding, " 'Cause I might want to donate parts to medical science for research." He was pleased with himself.

"Oh, that's perfectly okay. All science needs for research is certain key organs — eyes, heart, liver. There's still plenty of good rump meat left for the dogs. We'll just use the rump meat."

"Well, I don't know. My relatives might get upset."

"Don't worry, I'll pay them off. I'll buy the rights to your body. Trust me. They'll be thrilled. So do you mind if we use you for dog food?"

Doubtfully, "I guess I don't mind."

But we both knew he did.

That's what happens when people are not really sure what they believe. They believe whatever is the most convenient at the moment, until suddenly that belief becomes inconvenient. Then they get confused.

Desperately Seeking...Nothing!

Does your average teenager ever stop to consider the question of God's existence? Is it even a relevant subject? I used to think so, till Tom and Benson showed up at the yeshivah one day. They were backpackers, strolling around the world in sandals, looking for "the truth."

They were both real nice guys and really earnest.

I gave them some cookies and a drink, and we chatted. They told me all about their travels, and finally I asked, "Do you guys believe in God?"

Tom said, "No, sir, we don't."

Benson yelled out, "I sure do, Tom. Speak for yourself."

The two argued for a few minutes about whether or not they believed in God. But one thing was clear: they had never discussed the issue.

Many people often make proclamations about what they do and do not believe. "I believe there is a God," or "I believe there's no God." But the truth is that many of them have never even thought about it for more than a minute or two.

Flying Blind

When I was a student at Ohr Somayach, the yeshivah arranged for us to visit an Israel Air Force base and play basketball against the air force team. We had a pretty good team, with a couple of former high-school and college players, and we were confident that we could beat them.

We were going to make a *kiddush Hashem*, showing that not only did we have them beat in a spiritual sense, but that we would defeat them very soundly and effectively in a physical way. We'd top them in basketball, too.

Unfortunately, on that particular day we had to settle for spiritual superiority. In the physical realm they came out on top.

After the game we met the base commander, and he told us an interesting thing. He said that a pilot flying an F-15 fighter is moving so fast that at a certain point he cannot distinguish between the earth and the sky. Essentially he doesn't know which way is up and which is down. This, of course, can make flying a fighter jet a rather dangerous pursuit.

The only way for the pilot to discern up from down is by an indicator that tells him which direction he's flying. The pilots are taught to put total trust in that indicator — and they do.

I've thought about that a lot since then. Here is a human being, flying much faster than the speed of sound, and he must set his own instincts aside and rely completely on a computer.

It is a metaphor for life. Often, when rushing through life, we lose any sense of direction or purpose. At that time it's helpful to know there is a built-in indicator. It's called the Torah.

But it's like the onboard computer. For it to work, we've got to set aside our own instincts and place our uncompromising trust in the indicator.

An Absolute Maybe

People today are so sure they don't believe in anything that they don't even feel obliged to actually investigate what it is they don't believe in. They are cynics without the requisite background to be cynical. At least in the old days, before a person rejected religion, he went to the trouble of finding out something about what he was rejecting and convincing himself he was doing the right thing from a logical standpoint. Today a person need only watch a few movies, read a *Time* magazine article or two, and he's become a full-fledged atheist, no study required.

A quick-witted colleague told me a story that reflects this self-assured ignorance. This rabbi travels the world lecturing on Judaism and is subject to a lot of wearying air travel. The following occurred while he was flying from Australia to the United States.

Taking advantage of the long flight, the rabbi pulled out a travel-sized Gemara and began learning.

His seatmate, a young woman, said to him, "Excuse me, but is that a Talmud?"

"Yes, ma'am, it is. Why, are you Jewish?"

"Yes, I am, but I don't believe in any of that religious stuff."

"Really? Why not?"

"I don't believe in absolutes."

"Really? Are you absolutely sure?"

Here Today, Gone Tomorrow

Sometimes a little elementary logic is all it takes to make one's point.

Shawn had come to yeshivah after having studied to become a rabbi in a Reform college. He was obviously not satisfied with the Reform platform, but he wasn't quite ready to embrace Torah Judaism. As a compromise, he came to an Orthodox yeshivah, hoping to square his conflicting beliefs.

Shawn was desperately trying to hang on to a home-grown ideology that was somewhere to the right of Reform but still way to the left of Orthodox. One day he engaged me in a discussion regarding the obligatory nature of halachah. Shawn didn't feel halachah was binding, while I — no surprise here — did.

After the usual back and forth, I said to him, "What would happen, Shawn, if one day your son would ask you, 'Dad, what makes me Jewish?' "

Shawn said, "I would answer, 'Because your mother is Jewish.' "

" 'Well, Dad, my feeling is that the halachah that says I'm Jewish because my mother is Jewish is not binding, and therefore I'm not Jewish, and therefore I'm going to McDonald's.' What would you tell your son, Shawn?"

Hmm...uh...," shifting back and forth, "I guess he'd be right. If he doesn't feel it's binding, then he's not Jewish."

"Okay. Now the next day your son tells you that he is Jewish because he converted, and, by the way, as a Jew he'd sure like one of those nifty Chanukah presents. Of course, he didn't go to the mikveh or to a rabbi, because he doesn't feel that that halachah is binding either. What do you say then, Shawn?"

A little more hemming, a lot more hawing. "Uh, yeah, I guess then he'd be a Jew according to everyone's opinion."

"Uh, uh, uh! Not so fast, Shawn. You see, the next day he tells you he's not Jewish, because the halachah that says a Jew is a Jew forever, well, that one's not binding either. What then, Shawn?"

"That would be ridiculous. I'd put my foot down and make him decide."

"But, Shawn, that would be inconsistent. The kid's right. Nothing is binding, so he can change his mind daily."

"Okay, I agree. It's inconsistent." Shawn realized the absurdity of a nonbinding halachah and gave in graciously. It worked that time.

Shawn stuck around yeshivah for some time, learning with a *chavrusa*, and while I don't know where he is today or if he remained observant, I hope that he was left with some positive impressions from his stay here.

There's No "I" in Team

Of course, how much time could anyone spend pondering religion when everyone's so busy chasing the American dream?

I was shmoozing with one of my students, a boy named Michael Zaks.

"So, Michael, what's your goal at this stage of your life?"

"Well, Rabbi, you know I play the tuba for the Ohio State University marching band. At half-time of the Ohio State–Michigan game, the band forms the words 'Ohio State' on the football field, and the senior tuba player gets to dot the *i*. My goal is to dot the *i*."

I didn't say anything, but I thought to myself, *Wow, that's quite an ambition. What a shallow, empty life one must have if one's supreme goal is to dot the i. I mean, what comes after that, crossing the t?*

I thought about it later and realized how appropriate that goal is for today's world. In Hebrew the word for "dot" is *dagesh*, which means "emphasis." So "dotting the *i*" means putting the emphasis on the *I*, on me. Indeed, an appropriate characterization of the philosophy of today's Me Generation.

Oh, Yeah? Prove It!

Here is another message I try to convey.

A word on proof: Many books have been written on the divinity of Torah, advancing strong arguments proving that the Torah is divine and with advice on how to prove it to a nonbeliever. However, a cautionary word will save you from quite a bit of potential heartache and frustration.

When someone asks for proof, in any area, your first response has to be "Define proof." If you do not get him to first set the parameters of the required proof, then no matter what kind of evidence you present, the almost inevitable response is "Well, that doesn't prove it."

So when the typical skeptic — and we've all met one — says, "If you can prove to me one hundred percent that there's a God, then I'll accept Him," don't try to respond to such a person with normal rationale. You'll just be wasting a lot of valuable time. Anything you tell him will be met with a clever rejoinder and a dismissive "Oh, please, that doesn't prove anything." For this person, anything short of God doing a personal miracle for him right this minute will not suffice. And even then, who knows? But if you've made him set the criteria of proof, then he is at least bound by his own definition.

So if, for example, someone tells you, "The existence of God cannot be proven," don't start throwing all your carefully constructed answers at him, because he'll always find some loophole in your response.

This is not by accident. Chazal tell us that God always leaves enough room for doubt. If a person wishes not to believe, he is able to rationalize why it is justified. If there were no way to disbelieve, that would be a contradiction to the very concept of *bechirah*, free choice, and would undermine the major underpinning of man's creation.

Therefore you must insist that your challenger first define the logical parameters of what he considers proof with regard to any ordinary situation. Only when he has done so should you bring out your carefully researched proofs and arguments regarding the area under discussion. Otherwise you're in for a frustrating encounter.

The Mugging of Joe

Joe was a bright fellow. When I met him, he was in Israel on the Birthright program, which affords Jewish students the opportunity to visit Israel and get to know the land of their ancestors.

Originally from Chicago, Joe had once been Modern Orthodox, but he gave it up upon discovering Humanism. Humanism is a convenient thing to believe in, since it basically means that one can believe whatever one wants, and everyone else is enjoined to respect those beliefs, with absolutely no criticism allowed.

Officially a Humanist is someone who respects all other humans and doesn't judge them or their actions, but in practice it's even more flexible than that.

The best thing about it, from Joe's point of view, was that it was absolutely fair and unprejudiced, since its basic tenet was that all humans are good. Who could argue with a belief as nice as that?

I met Joe late one night at the dorm where he was staying, and, along with one of my friends, we had a long, comprehensive bull session until the wee hours, shmoozing about everything under the sun. We talked about religion and sports and politics and more.

Joe was obviously very bright, and I wanted to get him to try out a few months of learning in a serious yeshivah. The problem was, Joe already had his beliefs. Humanism. He believed that humans were good and wanted harmony with one another, and organized religion ruined that natural sense of loving-kindness. He felt the world would be better off without religion, which he saw as just a way of controlling people's lives.

Nothing I could say would dissuade him of the naiveté of his beliefs. I tried to explain to him that the Torah is not about controlling lives; it is a way to true Humanism, to helping people really become good and really live harmoniously. I told him that if a person did not work on his personal character traits, he could never achieve perfection.

But it fell on deaf ears. Joe was convinced that he was good, that he loved all humankind, and he didn't want the Torah interfering with his beliefs. To him the worst thing in the world was control of any sort over human beings. If left to their own devices, they would almost always behave themselves. A true liberal.

I told Joe what they say, that a liberal is just a conservative who hasn't gotten mugged yet. He smiled, but declined to agree.

During our conversation, one of Joe's fellow students came along and threw a bag of smelly laundry into another guy's lap, saying, "The washing machine is free now."

The boy jumped up, grabbed the laundry, and smacked the first guy with it. At first it looked like a game, but it soon became clear that this was an argument that had begun long before the laundry toss.

As the fight escalated into shoving, then punching, Joe, who was a big fellow, jumped up and tried to break it up. He grabbed one of the combatants, who thought Joe was part of the fight and turned on Joe with a fury, tearing his shirt and scratching him deeply.

It was beginning to look dangerous, so the dorm counselor and I helped break up the fight, each of us attempting to calm down one of the boys by talking to him gently. It wasn't easy. I'll spare you the gory details, but every few minutes one of the combatants would try to break away and continue fighting.

I talked to Joe, and he kept saying that the other guy was "really psycho and a menace to society." He said, "These New Yorkers are all crazy. You try to help them out, and they attack you."

Seeing that this would take time to sort out, I said goodbye to Joe and his friends and went home for the night.

The next day I saw Joe at Ohr Somayach, where he came to learn every morning. In the light he looked pretty beat up. His glasses were hanging crookedly, and his face was scratched up. I went over to say hello, and he started in again with the New Yorkers.

I said to him, "Boy, Joe, for a liberal Humanist you sure are prejudiced!"

He smiled sheepishly and said, "Yeah, Rabbi, I guess I finally got mugged."

— E. M.

Uniform Reactions

UNIFORM REACTIONS

I always try to make it clear to *ba'alei teshuvah* that as soon as they change their clothing and adopt a religious mode of dress, they assume a certain responsibility. Like it or not, they are being watched, focused upon. By donning black pants, white shirt, yarmulke, and tzitzis, they become a lightning rod for people's reactions and criticisms, fairly or unfairly.

As Orthodox Jews, they now represent the collective Jewish conscience, and they are, even by their very existence, going to rub somebody the wrong way. So they must be extra careful not to act improperly, even if the identical action performed by someone attired in jeans and a T-shirt would go unnoticed.

This phenomenon obviously applies to FFB's as well as *ba'alei teshuvah*, but when a person has been *frum* his entire life, he usually accepts this as a matter of course. He has been trained since childhood to always act with decorum in public and to try to create a *kiddush Hashem*, a sanctification of God's Name. A *ba'al teshuvah* may find it hard to fathom the extent to which his every action will now be scrutinized and must therefore be warned of this.

Ah Sukkaleh Ah Kleine

I use this gem of a story, heard form Rabbi Avraham Alter, to make this point.

David Brenner was one of those guys who get voted most likely to succeed in their school yearbook. Personable, handsome, and smart as a whip, he could have made it in anything he tried. But early on he set his sights on a life — I hate calling it a career — in the rabbinate.

He studied diligently, was accepted to a top *semichah* program, and burned the candle at both ends to complete his *semichah* with top commendations.

Now it was time to look for a position. David could probably have secured a well-paying job in a prestigious Orthodox or Modern Orthodox congregation; he certainly didn't lack for offers. But he had his heart set elsewhere. He wanted to serve a community that really needed strengthening, where he could really make a difference.

So he applied to synagogues that were lower down on the observance scale, but would still be willing to accept a religious rabbi. And he seemed to have found it. Congregation Beth Samuel in Lakeville, Connecticut, was a Conservative temple, but there were elements in the shul who felt they could handle a rabbi with a more "conservative" outlook; in other words, an Orthodox rabbi.

To make a long story short, David applied for the Lakeville post, was invited for a Shabbos audition, and completely won over the congregation. They loved his charisma, his speaking ability, and his obvious erudition. The board was also impressed with his plans for the synagogue youth, ideas for fund-raising, and suggestions for membership drives. The job was his.

David agreed to take the position, but he made one stipulation, something his own rabbi had stressed as being critical: there must be a valid *mechitzah*, a separation between men and women during the prayers.

While still not customary at Conservative synagogues, *mechitzahs* are today becoming more and more common as the congregants recognize the practical benefit to their devotions when there is separation of the genders and as some Conservative rabbis drift rightward. There is still plenty of time for social mingling during the *kiddush* and in the hallway.

So David's request was not immediately rejected by the board, and after careful consideration and debate, they agreed to it. But the final approval needed to come from the synagogue president, an elderly man who had not been able to attend the board meeting.

The meeting was adjourned with the tacit understanding that as soon as the president rubber-stamped the *mechitzah* request, David Brenner would become the new rabbi of Congregation Beth Samuel.

The next morning David received a call from the board chairman. "Rabbi, I'm very embarrassed to tell you this, but the president has rejected the *mechitzah* idea, and nothing I could say would change his mind."

David was shocked and asked if he could meet the president in person. Perhaps he could win him over to the idea.

The president received him cordially, but emphatically refused to consider the *mechitzah*, and nothing David said could budge him on the issue.

Finally David said, "Sir, would you at least tell why you are so set against this?"

"Certainly," answered the president. "I live next door to an Orthodox Jew. Every year for the past twenty-five years, I've watched as he built his sukkah in his backyard. I myself don't build a sukkah, but I would certainly appreciate the opportunity to pay a visit to one. Never once, in twenty-five years, has he invited me into his sukkah to share some holiday spirit. If that's what Orthodoxy is, then I'm not interested."

David Brenner did not get the job, the shul did not get the *mechitzah*, and the community did not get the benefit of this dynamic young rabbi and all he could have accomplished. All because one person was too shortsighted to realize what a little outreach could accomplish.

That's a heavy responsibility.

What a Ride!

Of course, as great as the responsibility is, so is the opportunity. A little *menschlichkeit* by a religious Jew goes a long way.

Nowadays we take for granted that there are yeshivos and seminaries for *ba'alei teshuvah*, *kiruv*-oriented summer camps, lunch-and-learns, campus outreach rabbis, and all sorts of programs designed to reach out to the unaffiliated and uninformed Jew.

We also take for granted the very phenomenon of *ba'alei teshuvah*. I personally have taught classes in a mainstream school where many of the students were children of *ba'alei teshuvah*. It has become so common that we rarely stop to wonder when this societal phenomenon began, or even if it had a beginning. Perhaps there were always tens of thousands of *ba'alei teshuvah*.

But the reality is not like that. When I was child, a *ba'al teshuvah* was a rarity, something to be marveled at.

"How did he become *frum*?"

"Where is he from?"

"His accent is a little funny."

"Why did he become *frum*?"

People would whisper and speculate, not in a sneering way, but with a sense of wonderment, like that experienced when a twenty-foot stretch limo would roll by in our religious neighborhood. It was unusual, something that attracted attention.

There were not a lot of people working in *kiruv*, and there were barely any organized options available to those individuals who were inspired to learn about their heritage.

Only in the seventies did Yeshivas Ohr Somayach open its doors and the so-called *ba'al teshuvah* movement really took off. One of the prime movers of the *ba'al teshuvah* movement, a man who influenced countless thousands of Jews to return to their roots, and who through his books is still influencing people today, was Rabbi Aryeh Kaplan. He was a brilliant individual, who, besides being a colossal Torah scholar, was a world-class physicist and was familiar with, quite literally, all academic subjects, from science to literature to astronomy and everything in between. His broad knowledge held people spellbound, and his warm heart demonstrated for them even more powerfully the beauty of being a Torah Jew.

When Reb Aryeh was eighteen, he heard a rabbi speak about the beauty of Torah and the Jewish lifestyle, and he decided to check it out for himself, to see if it might be for him. He enrolled in a yeshivah and began learning about Judaism, but for some reason he was not connecting, was not "feeling it." Aryeh determined that this was not for him; certainly it did not warrant derailing an already promising career as a physicist.

One Friday he told his roommate, "Moshe, I've decided that this isn't for me. This will be my last Shabbos in yeshivah. I'll be leaving early Sunday morning."

Shabbos came and went, and no, I'm sorry, no miraculous change came over him. He still didn't "feel it" and was beginning to realize that this was not the life for him.

On *motza'ei Shabbos* he packed his bags, thanked the rabbis for their assistance, and said goodbye to his roommate. On five o'clock Sunday morning he woke up and quietly slipped out of bed, doing his best not to wake his roommate. But his caution was unnecessary. His roommate was already up and dressed.

"Moshe, what are doing up so early?"

"I figured I'd drive you to the train station. It'll be hard to get a cab at this hour, and the buses haven't started running yet."

"But I'm leaving yeshivah. Why would you do this for me?"

"So you're leaving yeshivah. Does that make you less of a human being? I can still do you a favor."

When Reb Aryeh heard this, he stopped in his tracks. If the Torah could make such a mensch out of a young teenager, then there had to be something there that he just wasn't getting. He decided to remain in yeshivah and investigate his heritage a little more. This time he got it. He became a fully committed Jew and went on to benefit thousands of other searching Jews throughout his life.

All because of a thoughtful roommate.

When in Amish Town, Do as the Amish Do

We've all heard the famous story of the chassid who was accosted on the train by a nonreligious Jew and was raked over the coals for his antiquated mode of dress. In a two-minute diatribe, this chassid found out that he was an embarrassment to the Jewish people and a relic and a major cause of anti-Semitism.

When his attacker paused for breath, the chassid said, "I'm sorry, sir, I didn't mean to offend you with my dress. I'm Amish, and this is the way my father dressed, and his father before him. I am only doing as I was taught."

Now it was the other man's turn to be embarrassed. "Oh, I'm so sorry. I didn't realize… Please forgive me. I actually think it's wonderful that in the face of all this modernity, you stick to your tradition and you don't let the world influence you."

Hypocritical or not, this sort of encounter has been repeated hundreds of times by self-disdaining Jews who do not wish to be reminded of where they come from.

Oh, these Jews love tradition, as long as it's confined to Dutch Pennsylvania, the Amazon River basin, or, even, Meah Shearim. Then it's quaint and harmless. They'll even go visit tradition, armed with their trusty Minoltas and their sun hats. But please, please, don't invade the "real" world with your long coats and black hats. It embarrasses us enlightened Jews.

Well, as much as we'd like to oblige these people, and stay in our own "kosher" neighborhoods, and trust me, we would really prefer to stay at home, the demands of modern life, and particularly *kiruv*, require that we do join the "real" world occasionally.

And the reactions we encounter, especially from non-Jews, are often surprisingly positive and respectful.

We're in This Together

I was buying a coat in a gentile-owned shop. The proprietor was a well-dressed African-American gentlemen, and when he noticed my Orthodox-style garb, he said to me, "Now I do like those threads."

"Oh, thank you. I like your threads, too."

"Yup, I really like 'em. I'm not sure what you are, mister, but I'm a Seventh-Day Adventist myself."

Clothing sometimes speaks louder than words.

Men in Black

A prominent *rav* of my acquaintance was walking through a busy airport, conversing with a Catholic priest he had met on the plane, when he overheard a conversation taking place directly behind him.

"Hey, Bill, that guy on the left, with the black hat, what do you think he does?"

"I don't know for sure," answered his friend, "but I think both of those guys are in the same line of work."

Davening for Dollars

A well-known *rosh yeshivah* in Ashdod tells the following story.

A religious Jewish businessman was approached by a gentile acquaintance who worked with him in the same Manhattan office building.

The gentile said to him, "You know, I've always wondered why you Jewish guys are such good businessmen. I could never figure it out. But now I think I've got it. I see that every afternoon, for about ten minutes, you guys get together, and everyone stands quietly and thinks about his business. With concentration and focus like that, it's no wonder you guys do so well in business."

If only he knew the truth. We don't think about our business once a day; we do it three times a day!

Kind of Jewish

The first Jew in the history of the world was our patriarch Avraham, whose greatness is recounted in the Torah. The Torah tells us that his defining attribute, the one he perfected above all others, was that of kindness, of charity toward others. Our tradition tells us that this attribute, along with those of the other patriarchs, was passed down to the Jewish nation in an almost genetic chain of continuance. This is manifest today in the great amount of charity performed by Jews the world over.

This benevolent attitude is evident not only in religious Jews, but also in those who have left their faith and abandoned the laws of the Torah. The greatest philanthropists on the world scene are almost invariably Jewish, way out of proportion to their numbers and their wealth. However, religious Jews go even further; they have made charity a veritable way of life. To them, it is not only something they feel good doing, but it is a specific religious obligation.

Apparently, this charitableness is something the world at large recognizes as well.

Kirk and Robert dropped by the yeshivah one day. They told me they were visiting Israel, and they wanted to study in the yeshivah. They didn't look, sound, or give the impression that they were Jewish, but I sat down to talk to them anyway.

After some small talk, I got down to brass tacks. "Tell me something. Are you guys Jewish?"

"Yup. We're Jewish, Rabbi."

My ears heard one thing, but my brain was saying to me, "No way are these guys Jewish."

"So where's your mom from, Kirk?"

"Oh, Pennsylvania Dutch Country."

Baranovitch, Lodz, Cracow, and the names of several other bastions of Judaism went through my mind. Pennsylvania Dutch was not one of them.

"Are you guys sure you're Jewish?"

"Well, actually, we're not. But we feel Jewish."

"Really. Why is that?"

"Well, Jews are very kind people, and we feel kind. So we'd like to be Jewish!"

I explained to them that we don't actively proselytize, and we can't make them Jews just because they feel kind. But I told them that if they ever do decide to pursue Judaism in a serious manner, then for their own good, and the good of the Jewish nation, they should make sure to find an Orthodox teacher and *beis din* and not go the Conservative or Reform route.

What was interesting was that they both felt that to properly express their benevolent sensitivities the place to go was the Jewish nation.

Bozo the Rabbi

On a trip to America, I stopped in a clothing store to buy a suit. Being an extremely classy joint, there were no individual dressing rooms, only shoulder-height changing stalls, one right next to the other.

While I was trying on a suit, I couldn't help but notice a very large African-American gentleman trying on a humongous clown suit in the adjoining cubicle. I usually try not to stare, but a six-foot, four-inch, three-hundred-pound Bozo the Clown was irresistible.

He caught me staring, chuckled, and said, "Hi, there, Rabbi. I use this to teach Sunday school. You could probably use one yourself."

I'm thinking of trying it.

The Arab Rabbi

Sometimes all people see is the clothes.

Yossi Lefkovich is a young man learning in *kollel* here in Jerusalem. One day he had an experience that we all must eventually encounter in this uncertain world.

His mother-in-law came to visit.

After a few days of showing the young couple what they were doing wrong, Mom said to her son-in-law, "Yossi, listen, I want to take a trip up to Tzefas, and I want a private cab. But please make sure that it is not one of those Arab drivers. I'm scared to go with them."

Yossi called his Arab friend Mussa and said, "Mussa, I've got a job for you. I need you to take my mother-in-law to Tzefas, but do me a favor and put on a yarmulke."

Make no mistake. Yossi loved his mother-in-law, but Mussa was cheaper than the other cabs and an old, trusted friend.

Sure enough, the next day Mussa showed up wearing a yarmulke and took Yossi's mother-in-law to Tzefas for the day. They returned late that night.

"So, Ma, how did you like the trip up to Tzefas?"

"Oh, it was terrific."

"How did you like the cab driver?"

"Oh, he was such a nice man. And a *talmid chacham*, too!"

Hare Krias Shema

One of the hardest things to overcome is the self-consciousness one feels when davening in public places, such as airports and airplanes.

When I first began traveling, I would usually try to find an unused corner of the airport and hurry through the *tefillah* as quickly as possible, cringing every time someone walked into the area.

This all changed in Newark Airport. I was waiting for a flight when a huge group of bald guys wearing orange robes and sandals came dancing by, singing and chanting. I had an epiphany: they weren't hiding from anyone.

That's when I decided, if they're not self-conscious, than I certainly don't have to be.

A Real Maven

I was davening on an Olympic Airways flight, and I noticed an elderly gentlemen staring at me throughout the prayers. When I was done, he leaned over and said, "I know what those are. They're phylacteries."

I politely agreed and asked him how he knew this. He pulled himself up and puffed out his chest. "Well, I've seen the movie *Yentl*. I know all about Judaism."

I guess that made him an authority. Now if he'd just rent *The Ten Commandments*, he could probably learn enough about Judaism to become a Reform rabbi.

We're supposed to be a light unto the nations, but somehow I don't think it's going to happen through *Yentl*.

My Name Is Not Ishmael!

A friend of mine named Avraham was on a long flight on TWA. The time came to daven *shacharis*. Unlike afternoon and evening prayers, which can be prayed with relatively little commotion, *shacharis* requires the donning of a tallis and tefillin, and Avraham was a little self-conscious about making a scene on the plane. He didn't want to attract everyone's attention, so he asked the stewardess if there was a place where he could have a little privacy in order to pray.

The plane was one of those older 747s, which had no passenger seating on the upper deck. The stewardess brought my friend upstairs and pointed to a little space behind the cockpit where he could pray undisturbed. The young man thanked her and began his devotions.

Suddenly the cockpit door swung open, and out stepped the pilot on his way to the washroom.

The first thing he saw was a swarthy bearded guy wiring himself up with some black cables. Edging his way back into the cockpit the pilot demanded nervously, "Who are you?"

Although under normal circumstances, one should not speak while putting on tefillin, my friend decided that the current situation warranted some explanation. He looked up sheepishly and said, "Oh, hi, don't be nervous. My name is Abraham, and I'm just praying."

A quick lesson on the difference between tefillin and TNT put the pilot's mind at ease.

It's too bad the pilot hadn't seen *Yentl*.

Hair Ye! Hair Ye!

Yoram, a student of mine at Ohr Somayach, was a long-haired Israeli-American who seemed to think he was some sort of throwback to the sixties-era flower children. He generally dressed in a very slovenly manner, bell-bottoms and a longish goatee completing the look. He came to mandatory lectures, but seemed to have very little interest in making any change in his life, what we called a "low energy" guy, always tired, dragging himself around.

Since Gemara *shiur* had a mandatory attendance policy, Yoram would show up to my class and even participate in the give-and-take. I began noticing that Yoram was actually very bright. The problem was just his total lack of energy and disinterest in taking on challenges. I felt that this was due, at least partially, to a weak self-image.

Basing my approach on the words of the Rambam, I suggested to Yoram that perhaps by changing his mode of dress to something a little more respectable, he would succeed in making himself feel more respectable.

I said, "Yoram, what's with the hair?"

"Rabbi, no one's ever got me to cut my hair."

"Yes, Yoram, that's kind of obvious, but what's the point? It doesn't even look very good."

"I'll tell you the point. The point is that all you 'blackies' have no individuality. You all wear the same uniform — dark pants, white shirt, black hat. I don't want to wear any kind of uniform, and this is how I express my individuality, my uniqueness."

I'd heard this before, so I said to him, "Look, Yoram, the fact that a person is able to conform is not always a sign of weakness. Sometimes it's just the opposite — it's a sign of strength. It's a sign that a person feels so confident in his individuality, in his real intrinsic worth, that he can remove his externalities, his individual features, and still retain his uniqueness. If a person is afraid to conform on the outside, he must not feel very unique on the inside."

Two days later Yoram got a haircut, and it turned out to be a milestone in his complete revitalization as a person.

When the extent of one's identity is the external, and one's wardrobe is all a person is, then external conformity is indeed a sign of weakness, a way of hiding in the crowd.

But with *Yiddishkeit*, it's the opposite — the uniformity of dress is our way of emphasizing the inner self and deemphasizing the external and is thus a sign of strength and confidence, a confidence that the real person inside measures up and need not hide behind ostentation.

Only if you don't believe you can cut it internally must you make an external statement.

Too Much Too Soon

William Neiman came from London. He was outstandingly brilliant and quickly moved up the ranks in learning. Besides his learning success, I noticed that William was changing his manner of dress. In rapid progression he went from casual college attire (T-shirt and jeans, both dirty) to preppy American to full-bore black, the so-called yeshivish uniform, complete with rapidly sprouting *peyos*.

Contrary to what one might think, I wasn't pleased by this transformation. To the contrary, I was somewhat dismayed by its rapidity. Most often, when such a complete change occurs so quickly, it is not a healthy sign.

When a person has lived his life one way for over twenty years and then suddenly becomes "*peyos* man," it is a sign of instability. It's almost as though the person is running away from himself, which is never the healthiest way to effect a change in one's lifestyle.

We kept our eyes on William, talked to him, but he wouldn't listen. He seemed to feel that he was superior to the other students and must move according to his own schedule. All our advice fell on deaf ears.

True to form, one day he just freaked out. He dropped the whole religion thing like a hot potato. He cut off his *peyos*, dug up his old T-shirts, and took off.

He was a classic example of too far, too fast.

In general, when I see one of the new students sprouting *peyos*, I make a deal with him. "If you don't cut off those *peyos* within a couple of days, I will pull them out manually."

I've never actually had to play barber, because most of the guys get the message and trim them by themselves.

The reasoning is this: Who told you to grow *peyos*? Did your rebbes tell you? Do your rebbes have *peyos*? Who told you this is an integral part of your growth in Judaism?

Whatever spiritual gains there are in having *peyos* are usually far outweighed by the losses. As the above story illustrates, the very act of trying to do too much at once can impede one's progress and sometimes halt it completely.

Then there's the problem of alienating one's family. For reasons of harmony, and practicality, it is important for a boy who is becoming observant to maintain a healthy relationship with his family. Growing *peyos* and wearing outlandish clothes do nothing to enhance family harmony and will only hinder one's religious development.

I always tell the boys to look at it from their parents' perspective:

"Six months ago Brad left home, a clean-cut American boy wearing jeans, T-shirt, and an earring. Now Baruch is here, an apparition in black, and everywhere you look there's something hanging and shaking — tzitzis, *peyos*. Why couldn't he just stick with the earring?"

Who needs this strife? There are enough sticky issues involved with becoming observant that there is no need to add another one.

This does not mean a boy shouldn't grow *peyos* and add to his Jewish appearance. A young man who has already adapted to *Yiddishkeit* and is now pursuing a path of Chassidus, where he feels his expression of *Yiddishkeit* will lie, by all means may grow *peyos*. However, it must be done in a considered, well-thought-out manner and not on a childish whim.

On a more subtle level, there is a danger of feeling prematurely self-satisfied and accomplished with one's achievements, when in truth the only real change that has been effected is a change in wardrobe.

As the prophet Yeshayah says, "Tear your hearts, not your clothes." God wants us to change our actions, not our wardrobe. Sometimes the trappings of piety can prevent a person from achieving real piety.

A Barefaced Truth

My grandfather, Mr. Elimelech "Mike" Tress, was a very righteous man, a great *oheiv Yisrael*. One of his closest confidants and mentors was the sainted Satmar Rebbe, one of American Jewry's greatest leaders. The Satmar Rebbe was a tremendous scholar, an extremely holy man, and a person who, in addition to his sterling personal qualities, possessed a keen insight and a penetrating wit.

Together the eminent Torah leader and the devoted lay leader performed many great services for the fledgling religious communities of postwar America and Europe.

On one occasion, upon witnessing the profound respect that the Rebbe accorded my grandfather, one of his chassidim asked, "Rebbe, why do you show this man so much respect? He doesn't even have a beard."

The Rebbe regarded the chassid for a moment and then replied, "You are right! When Mr. Tress will go to the next world, he will be asked by Hashem, 'Jew, Jew, where is your beard?' but you, my friend, when you get to the next world, the question will be, 'Beard, Beard, where is the Jew?'"

It's not the beard that makes the Jew, but the Jew that makes the beard.

— E. M.

ABOUT THE AUTHORS

Rabbi Dovid Kaplan is currently a rebbe and lecturer at Yeshivas Ohr Somayach, a lecturer for Arachim, a popular speaker at numerous seminaries, and a contributing writer for *Hamodia* newspaper. He also travels on the local and international speaking circuit. He is the author of *The Ohr Somayach Gemara Companion*, published by Targum.

Rabbi Elimelech Meisels, grandson of Elimelech "Mike" Tress, is the founder and principal of P'ninim Seminary and a lecturer at Seminar Yerushalayim. He formerly taught at Yeshivas Lev Yesharim and is a contributing rabbi to Ohr Somayach's far-reaching "Ask the Rabbi" Internet program. He is a graduate of Ohr Lagolah and a *musmach* of HaRav Z. G. Goldberg. Rabbi Meisels has written several well-received articles in *The Jewish Observer* and is editor and contributor of JLE's *Lifelines* e-mail Torah newsletter.